Bring out the
BEST IN YOUR HORSE

Bring out the
BEST IN YOUR HORSE

CAROLYN HENDERSON

J.A. ALLEN · LONDON

© Carolyn Henderson
First published in Great Britain in 2009

ISBN 978 0 85131 945 2

J.A. Allen
Clerkenwell House
Clerkenwell Green
London EC1R 0HT

www.halebooks.com

J.A. Allen is an imprint of Robert Hale Limited

A catalogue record for this book is available from the British Library

Design and typesetting by Paul Saunders
All photographs © John Henderson 2009 except for – 4.1, 4.2, © Heather
Moffett; 4.19, 4.20, © Myler; 4.23 © Parelli; 8.3, 8.4, © V-Bandz
Edited by Martin Diggle

Line illustrations by Maggie Raynor: the illustration on page 20 is reproduced
from the author's *Getting Horses Fit*; that on page 129 is reproduced from
Dressage as Art in Competition by permission of John Winnett

Printed by New Era Printing Co. Limited, Hong Kong

Contents

Acknowledgements

Thanks to my husband, John, for photographs; the J. A. Allen team of Lesley Gowers, Martin Diggle and Paul Saunders for editing and design; to Lynn Russell, for her patience and skill in transforming a hairy cob into a pin-up and to Clippersharp, Net-Tex Lynn Russell Range and Wahl for products used in the makeover.

Introduction

ARE YOU BRINGING OUT the best in your horse, or simply taking him for granted? It's all too easy to assume that he will never look as good or go as well as horses you see at shows or read about in magazines – but if you take a new look at the way you keep, school and present him, you could be in for some pleasant surprises and a more rewarding partnership.

That's where this book is designed to help. In some ways, the ideas it suggests are akin to giving your horse a makeover, though it's far from being a superficial approach. 'Makeover' is a real buzzword and you'll see it everywhere in magazines and on TV, as celebrity experts transform everything from houses to people. Although they often have great ideas, a lot of their techniques evolve around quick fixes. In terms of appearance, there are lots of quick fixes you can apply to your horse, as you'll see in the chapters on presentation, but there are also long-term strategies to help you achieve long-term benefits.

They might not enable you to turn a nice but unremarkable horse into a superstar – but then again, there is always that possibility. In every discipline, from showing to eventing, there are animals who, at some stage, most riders would have passed by. But all it takes is one person to spot the potential that might be hidden by hairy legs, an underweight or overweight frame and/or lack of muscle tone, and a nondescript horse can become something special.

This book isn't just aimed at riders who want to compete, though they should find plenty of ideas to help them boost their performance and results. Riding for pleasure is just as important and, by making the most of your horse, you'll get the maximum pleasure out of your relationship with him.

The first step is to learn how to assess him, as dispassionately as possible. The first chapter will help you do that and you'll be able to make a list of his plus and minus points. By working through the book, you'll then learn how to make the most of the good things and improve or disguise the not so good ones.

Some improvements, such as building up muscle in the correct places, will take months. Others can be achieved in minutes with nothing more than grooming and trimming tools; these, of course, are purely cosmetic and some people may regard them as unimportant. However, if you take pride in your horse's appearance and get him looking his absolute best, you're in the right frame of mind to take pride in everything else you do with him.

Although this is a wide-ranging book rather than one which concentrates on schooling, you'll also find advice on improving the way your horse goes. Again, this will enable you to get more pleasure from riding him and, if you want to compete, boost your performance. Whilst it isn't possible to achieve miracles – for instance, you can't turn a horse who dishes badly into one with straight, elevated movement – you can make a huge improvement in the quality of a horse's work by improving his strength, balance and self-carriage.

Ask yourself whether your horse is a pleasure to own or if there are things you put up with. Whilst no horse is perfect and even the quietest animal has a strong flight instinct, there is no reason why any horse should not have good manners. There is no reason why you should allow him to barge, tow you around on the end of a lead rope or refuse to pick up his feet.

Similarly, there is no reason why you should be a mere passenger on your horse. With patience and consistency, you can ensure that you are the one in control and that you have a happy, willing and responsive partner. This, too, will make riding more pleasurable and, just as important, help to keep you safe.

You will also find that if you need to sell your horse, presenting him in his best light will enable you to attract a wider range of potential buyers – thus giving you a better chance of finding him the perfect home and perhaps also realising a better price. Dealers know that first impressions are important, which is why the most successful will always ensure that horses are well presented.

So, take the challenge to bring out the best in your horse. Take a photo of him and, if possible, a video of him being ridden. Work through this book and assess him again in three to six months, depending on how much effort you have to put in. At the end of it, you may find that your unremarkable horse shows a remarkable improvement.

Chapter One

Assessing your horse

To BRING OUT THE BEST in a horse or pony you own, or to assess one offered for sale, you need to look at him dispassionately. That's not always easy, but it is a skill every owner needs – and it will prevent you from either undervaluing your own horse's potential or making a bad purchase decision. Having an 'eye for a horse' allows you to decide whether an ugly duckling could become a swan, or is only ever going to become a big duck.

There are four main areas to concentrate on: well-being, condition, conformation and movement, and manners. These are important not just for the sake of appearance, but to ensure that a horse is healthy and stands the best chance of staying sound. This statement may sound a little odd in the context of manners, but an ill-mannered horse is more likely than a well-behaved one to 'play up' in a situation that may put his welfare (and that of his rider) at risk, both on the ground and under saddle.

This chapter shows how to compare what's in front of you with the ideal blueprint; at the same time, it's important to realise that there is no such thing as a perfect horse – even if you're lucky enough to own or find one who is perfect for you.

You also need to remember that what is ideal for a horse doing one job is not necessarily ideal for another. To use some extreme examples, the 'born on the bit' conformation of a dressage horse who finds it easy to go in self-carriage would be a disadvantage for a racehorse who needs a longer, lower outline to travel at speed. Similarly, the upright shoulders that provide pulling power for a heavy draught horse are the last thing you would want to see on a riding horse; he needs sloping shoulders to allow him to move in a way that makes him comfortable to ride and reduces the concussion on his lower forelimbs.

If you're reading this book to make the most of your own horse or pony, don't put just *him* under the microscope. Once you have the guidelines in your mind, analyse every horse you see. A lot of knowledgeable people do this automatically and it can be great fun as well as a great education. If you get the chance, talk to knowledgeable people in all disciplines, from dealers

1.1 and **1.2** *right and below* Horses for courses – whilst sloping shoulders make for a comfortable ride, fairly upright shoulders give a draught or heavy horse his pulling power.

and racehorse trainers to showing judges and dressage riders, about what they look for and the compromises they are prepared to make.

'Ringside judging' of showing classes is another good way to hone your appraisal skills, though there are two potential pitfalls. One is that a judge can only assess the horses in the class, so if they are all mediocre, the winner is going to be the best of an ordinary lot. The only way to avoid this is to pick your educational shows carefully and find ones of a high enough calibre to attract only high-quality entrants.

The other pitfall is that unfortunately, there are still too many show animals who are too fat, even at top level. Again, different jobs impose different requirements and you would not expect a show horse to be as lean as one who is about to compete in a three- or four-star horse trial. However, 'show condition' is still sometimes merely a euphemism for fat. Fortunately, some judges have the courage to penalise overweight horses – usually because the excess weight has a detrimental effect on the ride – but a fat horse with good conformation under the blubber will still be placed higher than one in fitter condition but whose conformation is technically poorer.

Condition clues

As riders in different disciplines have different ideas of what constitutes suitable condition, it's important to be objective rather than subjective. The best way to do this is to use a condition scoring system, as outlined on the next page. Some people use a scoring system of 1 to 9, but this simpler version is more user friendly.

Many research sources on condition scoring include diagrams. Whilst these can be useful, they can also be confusing, as unless you are looking at extremes of condition it isn't always easy to relate a diagram to a three-dimensional horse. You also need to consider the type of horse you are assessing; for instance, the ribs of a thin-skinned Thoroughbred with a fine summer coat may be visible from some angles even when the horse is in good condition. Similarly, in cobs and heavier breeds of native pony, a relatively thick neck may be a natural feature of conformation – though you need to recognise the difference between this and pads of fat.)

1.3 A thick neck is a feature of this Konig pony's conformation.

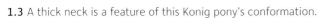

0 – Very poor. The rump is very sunken and there is a deep cavity under the tail. The skin looks as if it is tight over the skeleton, and the backbone, ribs and pelvis are all prominent. The horse will look as if he has a ewe neck (upside down) even when this is not the case.

1 – Poor. The above points apply, but to a slightly lesser extent.

2 – Moderate. The ribs are just visible, the neck is firm but narrow and the rump is flat either side of the spine. The spine itself is not visible. Ribs can usually be seen, though not obviously so as with the first two categories.

3 – Good. The ribs can be felt without applying undue pressure, but are covered. The rump is rounded and the neck is firm, but not cresty.

4 – Fat. There is a gutter along the back and rump and it is difficult to feel the ribs and pelvis.

5 – Obese. There is a deep gutter along the back and rump. The ribs cannot be felt and there are pads of fat, particularly on the crest, body and shoulders.

Whilst we will be aiming to see a horse scoring perfect 3s, somewhere between 2 and 3 is perfectly acceptable and a lean, fit racehorse or a top-level endurance or event horse (see photo 1.4) will be nearer 2. Compare the latter with the poor pony taken in by World Horse Welfare at its Norfolk head-quarters, who scores no higher than 1 (photo 1.5) and you'll see the difference between a horse who is lean and fit and one who has been starved; when the picture of the skewbald pony was taken, she was in foal.

1.4 This top-level event horse is a prime example of one who is fit for the job – a real cross-country machine.

1.5 *above* This poor in-foal mare, in starving condition, was taken in by the international charity World Horse Welfare. Sadly, she had so many problems that she did not survive.

Bodyweight is a major part of the condition picture, but not the only part. You also need to look at your horse's demeanour and at the state of his coat and hooves. Is he interested in life, or permanently dull and listless? Is his coat in good condition for his lifestyle and the time of year? Do you follow a correct worming programme which suits your horse and his surroundings? Are his hooves in good condition, or are they weak and crumbling? If in doubt, consult your vet.

Make and shape

Analysing your horse's conformation will enable you to make the most of him in two ways. First, it will help you understand what sort of work he is likely to find difficult. From there, you can decide how to help him overcome those difficulties within the limits his conformation imposes. For instance, a horse with insufficient space behind the jawbone naturally holds his head in front of the vertical and will find it difficult to flex and soften through the neck. He will be able to do so, to a limited degree, but it will take time, patience and correct schooling to improve his engagement and allow him to work as well as the limits of his conformation allow.

Also, when you've identified plus and minus points, you can, for showing and other purposes, draw attention to or, to some extent, disguise them through clever presentation techniques, as explained in chapters 9, 10 and 11. Sometimes, it's a case of what you *don't do* as much as what you *do*. For example, quarter marks draw attention to well-muscled quarters and good second thighs, but would not complement a horse with a weaker back end.

If you're not used to assessing conformation, or find it difficult to look at your own horse with a dispassionate eye, it may be easier to take photos. Looking at a photo rather than the real thing often helps you to distance yourself – but make sure they are good photos, as the camera can actually lie. Whether posing for a photo or being assessed in real life, the horse should be positioned on level ground as if you were presenting him for a showing judge: he should be on a loose rein or lead rope, with his head on or very near to the vertical and his legs slightly apart, so you can see each limb.

Study him, or take your reference photos, from each side and from the front and rear. Start with an overall impression before making a detailed analysis – does he present a harmonious picture, with everything in proportion, or is something not quite right?

If you already own and like a horse who does not match up to the ideal blueprint, don't worry. For a start, as mentioned, there is no such thing as a

1.6 Standing up a horse in this way makes it easier to assess his conformation – which in this case, is excellent.

perfect horse – and unless his minus points are particularly exaggerated, you'll be able to compensate; the only exception is if you have ambitions in top-level showing, when, no matter how well schooled the horse and how good a ride he gives the judge, bad conformation will inevitably see him down the line.

It's also important to look at your horse as a whole, because sometimes a minus can be compensated for by a related plus. For example, a horse who is rather short in the neck and also has an upright shoulder will usually have an up and down action that makes him uncomfortable to ride and the rider will feel as if there is nothing in front of him or her – but if a short-necked horse has a good slope to the shoulder, this will compensate the rider for the lack of length in the neck.

Ideals

Ideally, the length of a horse's head should be the same as the length of his neck; the depth of the girth should be the same as the length of his legs and his height should be the same as his length from his shoulder to the end of his croup. As we all know, ideal and real rarely coincide, but keeping these proportions in mind can help.

Head and shoulders

The *basic shape* of a horse's head is the least important part of his conformation, as so much can be done through presentation and choosing a bridle with proportions that complement him. However, the way his head is set on to his neck, the shape of his neck and the angle at which it comes out from the withers need to be considered.

As mentioned earlier, you really need enough space behind the jawbone for the horse to be able to flex easily. Horses with short, thick necks, such as cobs, are prone to failing in this respect and because their windpipes can be restricted when they are asked to work in a rounded outline, they may 'make a noise' in such posture.

A horse with a ewe neck, which looks as if it is set on to the withers upside down, is also unable to flex properly and, since the cervical vertebrae are a continuation of the spine, will often go with a hollow back. This, in turn, can lead to physical problems. However, true ewe necks are rare – in most cases, the horse simply lacks muscle on the top of his neck and/or has an incorrect build-up of muscle on the underside; the former being perhaps a lack of schooling/conditioning and the latter evidence of incorrect schooling. With time and correct rehabilitation work, these situations can be remedied.

If your horse's neck comes out of the withers at an angle which will assist in establishing self-carriage, it's a real plus point. This is something that breeders of dressage horses, in particular, strive for and is a selection point in the modern Warmblood. However, even a horse with a neck set on relatively low can be improved through correct muscular build-up, as long as the neck is not too short and heavy.

Defined but not over-pronounced withers help to keep a saddle in the right place. If you own a cob, you're probably asking, 'What withers?' They and many native ponies often have very little in the way of withers, so you need to compensate with the right design of saddle and choose a girth and numnah or saddle cloth that help with security without compromising the animal's comfort.

If your horse has the textbook sloping shoulders, you're halfway to a comfortable ride. Straight shoulder conformation predisposes him to an upright action rather than flowing movement – but unless the fault is pronounced, it may not be too much of a problem. Also, by making sure he works in balance and rhythm, you can make the most of his gaits, even if they aren't textbook perfect.

Body work

One of the classical textbook guidelines for conformation is that the horse's body should fit into a square. As with all ideals, variations only matter if they are extreme and views on what is ideal may vary slightly from discipline to discipline. Also, as disciplines evolve, so do the demands they place on horses. At one time, many top showjumping riders favoured short-backed horses because they felt they were easier to ride through combinations. Now, courses have become bigger and more technical and the pendulum has swung against the short-backed horse, who may find it more difficult to make the distances.

A markedly long back is a potentially weak point – the classic dealer's joke is that this is the sort of horse who can be ridden by all the family, i.e. one behind the other! However, a horse develops strength not so much through his back muscles as through developing the abdominal ones, so correct work can make a big difference to such a horse even if it can't compensate fully.

A dipped back can cause problems and many horses with this conformation naturally adopt a hollow outline. However, correct work and attention to saddle fitting can make a big difference. The same applies to a roach back, which has a convex outline: horses with this conformation often tend to be stiff-backed. Hopefully, your horse will have sufficient depth through the girth to provide plenty of room for the heart and lungs. In theory a shallower girth means the horse will not have as much stamina (as the horse is said to have diminished lung capacity) but there are plenty of eventers, endurance horses and even racehorses who don't meet textbook requirements but do excel in their jobs.

Look at a horse from in front and behind as well as from the side. From the front, you hope to see a chest that is neither too wide nor too narrow – though do keep the type of horse in mind when assessing this: a chunky cob will look wider than most Thoroughbreds, though both may be in proportion for their type. It's best to avoid extremes if possible, as a horse with 'both front legs coming out of the same hole' will often move badly, simply because his forelegs are too close together, and one who is overly wide will often have a rolling gait that is uncomfortable.

The horse's body behind the saddle is important – this is the engine, so it needs to be powerful. Although musculature can be built up through correct work, skeletal conformation defects will always remain. A horse with a big front and a weak back end, who looks as if he is two horses put together rather than having matching ends, will find it easier to pull himself along rather than work from behind, so will need careful schooling.

Look at a horse from all angles to see if he has an even build-up of muscle and if necessary, get veterinary advice. A horse who shows marked lack of muscle on one side, perhaps over one shoulder or one side of the pelvis, may have been worked incorrectly or may have suffered an injury. Rehabilitation work may make a huge difference, but you first need to find out the cause of the imbalance. Even if the horse seems sound, it is a good idea to ask your vet's advice.

Out on a limb

The horse world is full of pearls of wisdom. One of the best known – and most valuable – is 'No foot, no horse.' Foot and limb conformation must be judged together and it's often hard to know whether a problem is something you have to put up with, or whether it can be improved. The best people to ask for advice are your vet and farrier, but there are still points an owner can identify.

For a start, the size of the foot should be in tune with the size of the horse – you don't want to see pony feet on a big horse or soup plates on a little Thoroughbred. The feet should also form two matching pairs: the near fore should be a partner to the off fore and the near hind should match the off hind.

When you pick up a foot, the frogs should be well defined, the heels open rather than shallow and the soles slightly concave so they are less prone to bruising. Flat feet are particularly common in Thoroughbreds but a good farrier should be able to help this and most other problems.

Weak, crumbling feet are one of those problems that may seem minor until you own a horse who loses his shoes as fast as they are put on. Nutritional support and good farriery will help, but miracles are hard to come by.

The angle of the foot and the limb is very important if the horse is to move efficiently with minimum strain on joints, ligaments and tendons. There should be a continuous slope from the pastern down the hoof wall; the classical alignment is that the hoof/pastern axis should be about 45 degrees – the same as the ideal angle of the riding horse's shoulder. When the angle is broken, extra strain is imposed; this can be a consequence of conformation, or it can happen because the toes are too long and the heels too high, so get specialist advice and, if applicable, remedial farriery.

Limbs and feet have to stand up to a lot of stress, particularly when the horse is galloping or jumping. When horse people talk about 'quality limbs', they don't mean slender legs with no feather – they mean correctly proportioned limbs which withstand weight and work, whether they belong to a

1.7 Diagram showing the ideal slope of the shoulder.

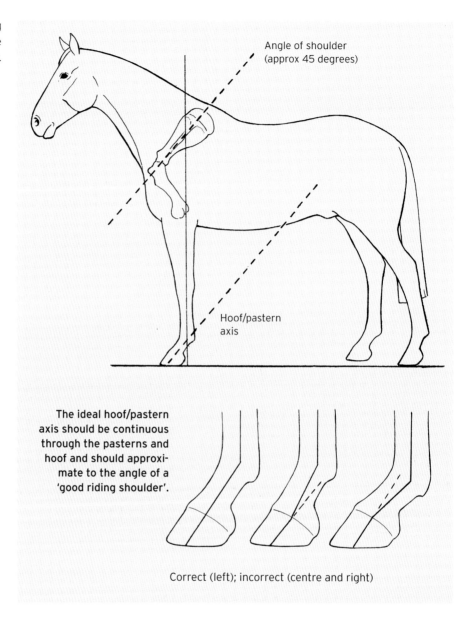

Angle of shoulder
(approx 45 degrees)

Hoof/pastern
axis

The ideal hoof/pastern axis should be continuous through the pasterns and hoof and should approximate to the angle of a 'good riding shoulder'.

Correct (left); incorrect (centre and right)

racehorse or a heavyweight cob. In front, the forearms should be long and the cannon bones reasonably short. The knees should be flat and wide and the cannon bones should not be offset.

When you look at the horse from the side, you don't want to see a markedly concave or convex outline between the knee and the fetlock. The first fault is referred to as being back at the knee and the second, as over at the knee. Both put extra strain on tendons and ligaments and many experts believe that, of the two faults, being back at the knee is the worse.

The horse's pasterns act as shock absorbers, so if he is to give a comfortable ride, they need to be reasonably long – but not so long that, as he moves, the fetlock drops so low that it puts too much stress on tendons and ligaments. Upright pasterns result in a jarring action and because the limb is less able to absorb concussion, the horse is more susceptible to problems such as ringbone. Hind pasterns are always slightly shorter than those of the forelimbs.

Hind legs are important, because they, like the hindquarters, are part of the horse's engine. In a horse who has been worked correctly, the second thigh or gaskin will be well muscled, but this may not be the case in one who has always been allowed to slop along or is too young to have done any proper work. This can be improved dramatically with correct schooling.

Hock joints should be wide, deep and not too straight. What is often described as 'well let down' hocks are stronger and more efficient than those which are too high. The commonest conformation faults in this area are cow hocks and sickle hocks; cow hocks, which turn inwards, like a cow's, are theoretically weaker, but there are a lot of good event horses who succeed despite this supposed weakness. Sickle hocks, where the lower leg is too

1.8 The horse's pasterns act as shock absorbers, as can clearly be seen here.

far forwards – sometimes to the extent that the horse looks as if he is about to sit down – are a definite weakness, as too much strain is put on the hock joints.

Lumps and bumps

If your horse is blemish free, you're lucky. However, although blemishes are unsightly, they are not of themselves unsoundnesses and you can disguise things such as small scars and even splints. Splints, bony enlargements on the splint or cannon bone, are caused by strain or blows and are usually found on the forelegs.

A capped hock has a fluid-filled enlargement on the point of the hock. Capped hocks are often seen in pairs and are usually called by a horse kicking at the walls or scraping his hocks as he gets up. Bog spavins and thorough-pins are also evidenced by fluid build-up; both may respond to veterinary treatment if caught early but are usually linked to poor hock conformation.

A curb is a swelling on the back of the leg, just below the hock. A true curb can be caused by strain of the plantar ligament in the hock, infection or tendon injury; a false curb isn't a curb at all and the horse simply has a lateral splint bone with a prominent head. A true curb won't disappear when you pick up the horse's hind leg, but a false curb will.

Windgalls – or windpuffs, as they are called in America – can be articular or tendinous. Articular windgalls are swellings on either side of the limb, between the back of the cannon bone and the suspensory ligament. Tendinous windgalls are seen just above the fetlock and are enlargements of the digital flexor tendon sheath. Both are blemishes and a sign of strain, but in some cases they can be reduced, at least temporarily.

On the move

The quality of a horse's movement isn't judged simply on whether or not he moves straight, though this is usually the first consideration. It's obviously an advantage if he is a straight mover, as marked deviation from the ideal puts stress on the limbs. However, unless you're concentrating on showing, a horse who dishes slightly – throws one or both forefeet to the side – or whose fore or hind limbs move slightly closer together than is ideal should not present a problem. In fact, if you take a look at international dressage and event horses, you'll see plenty whose movement isn't *perfect*, but is still of good quality.

However, a horse can move straight and still be unbalanced and/or lack rhythm when ridden. There are several possible reasons for this; for instance, he may be a young horse who is not yet established under saddle and is still learning to find his balance with the added complication of a rider's weight. An older horse may never have been taught to go correctly; to use his hindquarters and hind legs as his engine and push off from behind rather than pulling himself along with his forelegs. In fact, he may actually have been discouraged from doing this by incorrect riding. Incorrect riding may also spoil the quality of a horse's movement in other ways; for example, if he is winched in at the front end in an attempt to give a false impression that he is on the bit, he will be restricted through his whole frame.

Whilst you can never turn a horse whose skeletal conformation is such that he moves badly into one who moves well, you can do a lot to improve an 'average' way of going. This takes time and correct training, as a horse can only be truly on the bit when he has the muscles and strength that allow him to carry himself correctly. But watch any horse out in the field when he's first turned out, or when something catches his attention, and you'll often see him showing an elevated, rhythmical movement that would delight any dressage judge. They can all do it on their own – it's up to us to help rather than hinder them when we ride and train them.

Health checks

Is your horse healthy and comfortable? If you haven't had any particular problems with him, you might think this is a silly question – but a lot of people get so used to seeing their horse every day that, no matter how much they care about him, they take things for granted. They don't notice deteriorations in performance until they reach crisis point, perhaps because they happen gradually – a saddle that needs adjusting starts causing pressure points that are slightly uncomfortable, or the early stages of dental problems result in a horse hanging a little bit on one rein.

Similarly, whilst we can explain what it's like to feel a bit off colour and ask others to make allowances, your horse can't. If he's tired and lethargic because he's incubating a virus, it isn't fair to ask him to work, yet how many riders – and trainers – assume he's being lazy and that more forceful riding is the answer? Even worse, how many times have you heard someone say a horse is being 'naughty' or 'annoying' because he won't do something: perhaps canter on a particular lead?

A horse does not wake up and think, 'I really don't feel like schooling today, so I'm not going to canter on the right leg.' If you keep getting the wrong strike-off, it's because he doesn't understand what you're asking – or, for one reason or another, simply finds it difficult.

To allow your horse to perform at his best, whether he is a competition animal or a pleasure hack, it's essential to carry out regular checks and to constantly ask yourself if you're *allowing* him to do so. This means recognising the signs of a healthy horse, making sure you have essential healthcare in place and appreciating the importance of good farriery and correct, well-fitting tack. All these areas will mean calling in professional support – but you need to know when it's required.

To make the most of your horse, you need a good back-up team, comprising qualified professionals who will work not only with you, but with each other. You, your vet, farrier, saddle fitter and so on should be able to work together, but you need to be able to recognise when your horse needs them.

Signs of a healthy, happy horse

- A generally interested and alert attitude. At the same time, he should be relaxed in appropriate circumstances.

- Interested in food and showing a healthy appetite. Loss of appetite is often the first sign that something is wrong.

- A healthy coat appropriate to his type and the time of year.

- Eyes that are clean and bright, with no sign of discharge.

- Clean nostrils, with no sign of thick discharge – a small amount of watery discharge is normal.

- Droppings that are passed regularly and of the right consistency, neither cow pats nor hard balls. Remember that a flush of grass or excitement may result in looser droppings.

- Normal TPR (temperature, pulse and respiration) rates at rest. Temperature should be 37–38.5 degrees C (98.5–100.5 degrees F). Pulse rate should be 28–42 beats per minute and respiration rate 8–6 breaths per minute, with breaths smooth and unlaboured.

Monitoring the basics

Whilst it's obvious when a horse is seriously ill, it might not be so easy to spot when he is slightly off-colour. It's therefore important to know what is normal for your horse and to monitor him regularly so that you can catch signs such as a slight rise in temperature. On top yards, it's often standard practice to take and record each horse's temperature at the same time each day.

To take the pulse, feel for the facial artery under the jaw. Alternatively, feel for the heartbeat on the left-hand side of the chest, behind the elbow.

The easiest way to count the respiration rate is to stand slightly behind and to the side of your horse and watch the movement of his flanks. Each rise and fall counts as one breath.

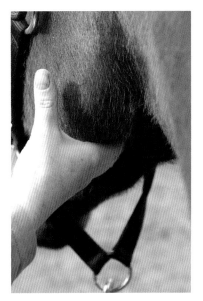
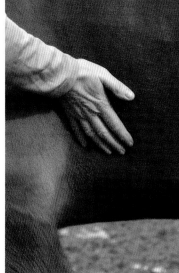

1.9 *left* Take the pulse by feeling the facial artery under the jaw.

1.10 *right* You can also feel the heartbeat by feeling the left-hand side of the body, just behind the elbow.

Feet first

Good hoof care is essential, whether your horse is shod or goes barefoot. In the past few years there has been a huge surge of interest in working horses without shoes and there are high-profile cases where this has proved remarkably beneficial – for example, UK racehorse trainer Simon Earle has achieved a remarkable turnaround in the performance of some horses who had previously experienced foot problems by running them barefoot, but it isn't an easy or necessarily cheaper option and may not be suitable for all horses and all conditions.

Whatever your situation and preferences, every horse should be seen by a qualified farrier every four to six weeks to ensure that his feet are correctly balanced. Even if it appears that shoes are not worn down excessively after six weeks, the feet will have grown. If they become too long, the horse is more likely to stumble, and structures in and around the foot will be under too much pressure.

Your role is to check and clean out your horse's feet daily, thus avoiding potential problems such as stones and other objects becoming lodged, or injuries resulting from loose shoes and infection starting because of a build-up of muck.

Dental care

If your horse has dental problems, he won't get the full value from his food and he won't be comfortable with a bit. This isn't rocket science, but it is something that's often ignored. Surprisingly, there are professional riders and trainers whose first reaction to a horse showing resistance to the bit – which can also be manifest by overall tension – is to use a tight noseband that literally keeps his mouth shut.

Common sense ought to dictate that the first step is to get him checked by a vet with an interest in and specialist knowledge of dental problems, or a qualified equine dental technician. This applies even if he has been seen fairly recently – and, of course, dental checks should be carried out on an annual or six-monthly basis depending on your vet or EDT's advice. My five-year-old suddenly started resisting on the right rein just three months after he had been examined, but a second examination showed that, in between visits, a cap from a deciduous tooth had been partly shed, but remained lodged. Once this was removed, full steering was resumed.

Worming

It's a fact of life that every horse carries parasites; however, you need to minimise your horse's worm burden with an approach tailored to his history and environment. Strategies may differ and it's usually best to ask your vet's advice. If you buy a horse with an unknown worming history, most vets will suggest that he is wormed immediately and will recommend appropriate drugs.

You can then combine faecal egg counts with targeted worming, which most people now agree is the most sensible strategy. Your horse's environment and your management will also affect the regime you need to follow: if you keep the same horses in a long-term home and pick up droppings daily, you will usually find that their worm burden is lower than that of horses on yards where the population changes regularly and pasture management is not as targeted.

A horse with a heavier than necessary worm burden sometimes, but not always, looks poor. Don't go by appearance alone: a horse can look healthy but still have a heavy worm burden.

Personality plus

Finally, don't discount your horse's personality! It's often said that a good show horse has presence – that as well as having good conformation and movement, he has that 'look at me' quality that catches the eye. However, this isn't limited to horses who can impress in the show ring: you'll sometimes see the most theoretically ordinary looking horse or pony who has 'something about him'.

There are also plenty of horses who look nothing out of the ordinary when they are in their stable or field, but are transformed when they work. This is down to a rider who has taught them to work correctly within the limits of their conformation and is a lesson to us all.

Just as important – or, perhaps, more so – is your horse pleasant to live with? You wouldn't want to share your life with someone who was ill-mannered, but a surprising number of owners are prepared to put up with horses who are just that. They let them tow them around on the end of a lead rope, barge, invade their space and assume that this is normal behaviour or something they have to put up with. It isn't!

Similarly, if a horse has never been taught to accept that being tied up, tacked up, having his feet picked up and so on is a normal and unthreatening part of life, he may react in a defensive way. If he associates these things with discomfort – if, for instance, he has been pinched by a girth or had his teeth banged by someone putting on his bridle in a hurry – he may not feel like co-operating, and who can blame him?

Serious behavioural problems should only be tackled with expert input and it's important to start by getting your vet to rule out physical causes. However, turning an ignorant but basically unspoilt horse or pony into one who is well mannered is a matter of common sense rather than mystique, as you'll discover.

Chapter Two

Muscles and movement

W HILST YOU CAN'T CHANGE YOUR horse's skeletal conformation, you can change the development of his muscles and, by doing so, improve his athletic capability, strength and performance. Through this process, you will also improve his appearance and, in some cases, the quality of his movement. However, it takes time – and unfortunately, that is something a lot of people are not prepared to allow. Do not be one of these people – be assured that *there are no quick fixes* and trying to produce instant results will result in a horse who is stiff, confused and even sour in his outlook.

Whatever you are trying to achieve, start with basic health checks. For instance, whilst everyone knows that dental problems can cause resistance to the bit, they can also cause muscular imbalance. If a horse carries his head to one side, or is consistently above the bit, he will move awkwardly and, in just a few weeks, this can lead to asymmetry.

Assessing musculature

The previous chapter should help you assess your horse's conformation and condition. You also need to look at his musculature, posture and demeanour to decide whether he is able to cope with the level of work he is being asked to do. Many of us are unfair to our horses without meaning to be; we complain that they are stiffer on one rein than the other without taking into account the fact that their current physical make-up doesn't allow them to be anything else. Yet most of us are either left-handed or right-handed – how many ambidextrous people do you know?

Most horses find it easier to work on one rein than the other and there are various ideas and opinions as to why this is so. Some people believe that it is related to which direction a foal curls in the womb, others point to rider imbalance and a third theory is that most riders find it easier to work their horses on the left rein because that is the one on which they are traditionally handled. It seems possible that some combination of all these factors is involved in most cases.

If a horse is seriously stiff or shows lame steps, it's important to check out physical causes, which must start with investigation by a vet. Sometimes, residual or secondary causes can be involved. For example, an old injury can leave a legacy of imbalance; discomfort from a badly fitting saddle can make a horse carry himself in a crooked fashion to try to relieve it. Also, a lopsided rider will produce a lopsided horse.

So – before you start trying to produce a muscled-up equine athlete, look at whether the muscle he's already got is in the right places and is evenly distributed. Starting at the front end, you want the top of his neck to be reasonably firm and to follow a slight arch, and the underside to be soft. If the muscle is on the underside of the neck, you may be told that the horse is ewe-necked – that his neck is set on 'upside down.' However, it's more likely that the horse habitually carries himself incorrectly, possibly because he is uncomfortable, but more likely through poor schooling, poor riding or a mixture of all three. The good news is that by sorting out the problem or problems, you can transform a horse's neck musculature and way of going – though it will take some time. Some breeds and types find it easier than others to work in self-carriage because of their conformation. For instance, Warmbloods who have been bred selectively for dressage are often 'born on the bit' whilst Thoroughbreds and Quarter Horses tend to have necks which come out from the withers lower down. The latter isn't a *fault*, because it, too, is an example of selective breeding: Thoroughbreds are bred to gallop as fast as possible, which demands a lower head-carriage than collected work, and Western riders also require a lower head-carriage in their horses.

This does not mean that horses with this type of conformation cannot be schooled to work on the bit and to carry themselves in an accepted 'dressage outline', as can be seen from many top event horses. It may take longer to build the strength in their hind legs and hindquarters to allow them to do it, but if they have the right kind of 'trainable' temperament, it is a very reward-ing process. Nor does it mean that horses ridden Western style are on their forehand; those who are correctly trained and ridden still use their back ends

2.1 Western-style riders require their horses to adopt a lower head carriage than, for instance, English-style dressage riders.

and lift their shoulders and a reining horse would not be able to perform advanced movements such as spins and sliding stops without engaging his hind legs.

Muscle atrophy at one or both sides of the withers is usually a sign that, at some stage, the horse has been or is being ridden in a saddle that does not fit and is causing pressure through the points of the tree. Most commonly, the tree is too narrow, but another or additional reason may be that the saddle is balanced incorrectly and is tipping the rider's weight forwards, again applying pressure over the tree points. See Chapter 4 for guidelines on fitting saddles and getting professional help.

Many horses have one shoulder that is more muscled than the other. The root cause can be either the rider sitting more to one side than the other or the horse carrying himself in a one-sided way – but this is a real 'chicken and egg' situation and means that particular attention must be paid to rider symmetry and saddle fit.

When muscles in the horse's back are underdeveloped, particularly those in the lumbar area, he will inevitably have slack abdominal muscles. It is only when the abdominals are strong and toned that he will be able to step under with his hind legs and lift his back. Even horses with naturally poor back conformation can be strengthened by careful schooling. In these cases, it's essential to get help from an expert saddle fitter with remedial experience and to accept that your horse will probably need regular check-ups and maintenance treatment from a qualified practitioner. You also have to accept that, whilst building the correct muscles may improve your horse's appearance, you will not be able to turn imperfection into perfection.

Look carefully at the muscles on your horse's pelvis. Make sure he is standing square, then stand directly behind him at a safe distance. If necessary, stand on a mounting block so that you can see whether he is muscled up equally on both sides of his pelvis, or if one side slopes down at a sharper angle.

At the same time, check whether the points of the hips are level, because if one is higher than the other, it often indicates that he has had an injury to the pelvic area. This could be a result of something obvious, such as a fall when jumping, or it may be related to an incident that you know nothing about, such as the horse getting cast or slipping over in the field.

At the same time as you study your horse's pelvis and hindquarters, see if he is equally muscled over his second thighs. Horses who have just started their education or who have never been schooled systematically will lack muscle in this area, as they will not be pushing off from their hind legs. You may also see horses who are noticeably more muscled on one side than the other. This, again, may be the result of an injury or it may be that the horse is weaker on one side than the other. If necessary, get your vet to assess him.

In addition to looking at them, feel the state of your horse's muscles, especially those in the back and saddle area. Run your hand firmly over and behind the area where the saddle sits, without digging in with your fingers. If your horse dips down to one side, or you feel his muscles tense up, he may be sore; if so, get veterinary advice and get the fit of your saddle checked. Don't confuse soreness with moving away from pressure and if necessary, get expert advice to ascertain the difference.

Groundwork

Building up your horse's muscles goes hand in hand with building up his fitness and, as he gets fitter, so he should become stronger in himself (see Chapter 6). However, a horse can become fit without becoming muscled *correctly*, so the best approach is a combination of ground and ridden work.

Groundwork can include lungeing, long-reining, stretches and massage. As stretches and massage are often incorporated in grooming routines, these are discussed in Chapter 9.

(It is assumed throughout this book that the horse you are working with has been backed and can be ridden in walk, trot and canter and that he understands the basics of being lunged. If you are not sure of his work history, it is recommended that you treat him as an unbacked horse and get help from a good trainer.)

Lungeing

Whilst lungeing is a great way of encouraging a horse to work correctly, it is physically demanding. The horse is working continually, on at most, a 20-metre circle (usually smaller than this) which means that his joints are working harder than if he were moving in straight lines. In particular, he is using his hock joints as his inside hind leg steps under.

For this reason, it's important to keep lungeing sessions short and to warm up the horse before asking for concerted effort. It's also important to keep your circles as large as practical. The textbook lungeing method which requires the trainer to stand on one spot is fine with a well-schooled horse, but doesn't work well with one who is inexperienced and/or less co-ordinated. In these cases, it's much better to walk a small circle yourself and to intersperse circle work with short intervals of moving the horse along the straight side of the school.

Lungeing a horse to work him correctly is different from lungeing purely for exercise, though you should never let a horse just whizz round on something resembling a circle. A lot of people do this, fondly believing they are improving his way of going and building up his muscles, when in fact they're simply letting off his energy and possibly increasing the strain on his legs. Remember that you can ask for half-halts and lengthened strides on the lunge, just as you can under saddle, and that you can also work on the quality of your horse's transitions.

Lungeing can be incredibly productive or incredibly boring. Don't forget that using poles on the ground can encourage your horse to lower his head and neck, look where he's going and ask him to lengthen or shorten his stride, depending on the distance between them. For an in-depth guide, read *Schooling with Ground Poles* by Claire Lilley (see Further Reading).

Not only do you need to think about the way you lunge, but also about where you do it and what equipment you use. You don't necessarily have to have an arena, but you do need a safe, enclosed area with a good surface in which to work your horse. You may be able to section off a reasonably level area of a field, but make sure that you aren't asking your horse to work on a surface that is too hard, too slippery or too uneven. Certainly, a well-maintained arena is ideal, but one in which the going is too heavy – for instance, if the surface is very deep – will make it difficult for your horse to work and will also increase the risk of injury.

Regarding equipment, it's common sense to fit brushing boots all round, in case your horse knocks himself. In most cases, it's best to attach the lunge rein to a lunge cavesson rather than directly to the bit ring as, if you're using auxiliary equipment which attaches to the bit, you won't then get blurred signals. However, if you're faced with lungeing a horse who is likely to get to the end of the lunge line and take off, you might need to start off by fitting the lunge line through the inside bit ring, over his head and attaching it to the outside bit ring. Photo 2.3 shows this set-up for lungeing on the left rein; to lunge on the right rein, you would pass the lunge line through the offside (right) bit ring, over the head and clip it to the nearside (left) bit ring. This gives more control but can also impose considerable leverage, so isn't recommended for general use.

Whilst leather lunge cavessons are ideal, they are also expensive and a well-designed nylon version is an adequate alternative. You may also want to look at the Rambo Micklem Multibridle, a very long name for a very good idea. Designed by Irish trainer William Micklem FBHS, this can be used as a bridle, a lunge cavesson which fastens below the bit – similar to the classical Wels cavesson – or a bitless bridle.

2.2 *below left* In most cases, it's best to attach the lunge rein to the lunge cavesson rather than to the bit ring.

2.3 *below right* Attaching the lunge rein this way will give you more control over an unruly horse. Here, it is set up for lungeing on the left rein.

2.4 The Rambo Micklem Multibridle fastens below the bit and in this context, is similar to the Wels cavesson.

Choose a lunge rein which is comfortable to handle. Some of the cheaper nylon ones are really not worth buying, because as well as being too lightweight, they can be uncomfortable to handle even when you are wearing gloves. The best ones are heavyweight cotton web, either plain or with grips down the holding area similar to those on Continental style reins.

Don't risk lungeing any horse without wearing gloves, even one who goes like the proverbial clockwork mouse. The day you take that risk is the day something will spook him and he'll pull the rein through your hand, which can be painful and a possible cause of injury. It's also best to wear a hat.

Most lunge work should be done in walk and trot. Cantering on the lunge is hard work and puts physical and mental pressure on a horse who is not fully balanced. Don't ask for this until the horse is confident and can stay in balance and rhythm when lunged in trot. However, if you're trying to improve the canter of a sound, established horse, short periods of canter work on the lunge may help, preferably using two reins (see section on long-reining) or an EquiAmi or Pessoa training aid, as explained in Other Training Aids, later this chapter.

Getting in shape

The first few minutes on the lunge, like the first few minutes under saddle, should be looked upon as a warm-up period, without attempting to influence the horse's outline. As a general guide, you can then ask him to work for up to 10 minutes on each rein, depending on his fitness and stage of training, then finish by cooling down for 5 or 10 minutes on each rein, again without auxiliary equipment.

Once your horse has warmed up, you need to encourage him to adopt the correct posture, which in most cases means using a training aid. This is where semantics can cause confusion, because once you use the term training aids, a lot of people automatically think in terms of draw reins and tying down the horse's head. Instead, take the name literally, because every piece of equipment you use should be an aid to training.

The logical way to build up a horse's muscles is to follow a three-stage plan, with each stage taking several weeks of lungeing, two or at most three times a week. First, ask him to stretch through his back and neck, which will strengthen his abdominal and back muscles. I think that by stretching the back muscles, you are also strengthening them. Next, ask him to adopt a more rounded outline, which will necessitate him 'lifting' his abdominal muscles and thus lifting his back. Once you have reached this stage, you can ask him to step under more with his hind legs, which in turn will lift his forehand.

This sequence is, of course, the same as that which should be followed in ridden training. However, because the horse is working without having to compensate for the rider's weight and only has to balance himself, he will find it easier.

Stage 1

Some horses realise from the start that they can stretch down on the lunge and they will do so simply when the lunge rein is attached to the centre ring of the cavesson. However, others need a little encouragement and the classical way to 'show them the way to the ground' is to use a Chambon. This applies gentle pressure on the poll and bit but because the cords or straps run through the rings on the poll pad rather than being fixed, the action is persuasive rather than demanding.

When you introduce a Chambon, it's best to fasten the cord clips to the rings on the poll pad (see photo 2.6) to introduce the idea of poll pressure. If the horse accepts this happily, you can then pass the cords through the poll pad rings and fasten them to the bit rings. When the horse is standing with his nose on the vertical, there should be no loops in the cords, but neither should his head be forced down. He will soon learn that if he lowers his head and stretches his neck, the cords will slacken and there will be no pressure.

Occasionally, a horse will resist a standard Chambon. In these cases, it's worth trying an elastic schooling rein, sometimes called a bungee rein. This is made from strong elastic cord incorporating a small amount of give, which is probably why a horse who doesn't answer the action of a Chambon will respond better. In many cases, if you use a bungee rein for a few sessions and then try a Chambon again, the horse will accept the latter quite happily. For this application, the bungee rein passes over the poll and through the bit rings and then goes between the forelegs to the girth (see photo 2.7).

2.5 *left* The Chambon is used to persuade the horse to stretch down on the lunge.

2.6 *below* When using a Chambon for the first time, introduce the idea of poll pressure by clipping the cords directly to the poll pad rings to begin with.

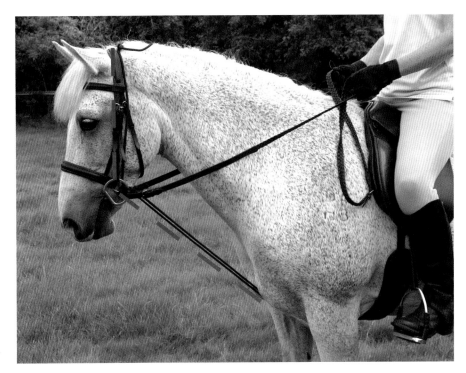

2.7 Some horses respond better to an elastic schooling or bungee rein, which can also be used when riding.

Stage 2

After a few weeks, your horse will have learned to stretch down and you will probably find that his stride becomes longer. The next stage is to ask him to work in a rounder shape and, to encourage him to do so, most people use side reins or an alternative.

Opinions vary as to whether plain or elasticated side reins are best. Some trainers believe that plain ones give the horse confidence to work into a relaxed contact, whilst others maintain that elasticated ones mimic the elastic contact we aim for as riders.

The best way to introduce side reins is to use just one, fastening it on the outside – so if you intend to start lungeing on the left rein, fit a side rein on the right-hand side. If you don't know the horse well, you may wish to err on the side of caution by attaching it to the side ring of a lunge cavesson first, then, when you have lunged him for two or three circuits, clip it to the snaffle ring. Start by fastening it fairly loosely – but not so loose that it flaps around and makes little jerks on the bit – then adjust it so that there is a light contact when the horse's nose is just in front of the vertical.

Using just an outside side rein, with the lunge rein fastened to the centre ring of the cavesson, can help encourage a horse who is reluctant to take a contact on the outside rein, as he doesn't have the option of 'leaning' on the other one. In most cases, when a pair of side reins is fitted, they should be of equal length. However, if you're having problems getting a correct canter strike-off in your ridden work and are sure it is not a result of incorrect riding, adjusting the inside rein a hole or two shorter than the outside one may help. Remember to alter the side reins when you change the rein, or you will be asking the horse to bend the wrong way.

With some horses, it's difficult to achieve good results using ordinary side reins even when you are using your body language and positioning the whip correctly to send the horse forward. Their advantage, which is the fact that they remain stable whatever the horse does, can also be a disadvantage if the horse resents their fixed nature. If, despite your best efforts, a horse persistently comes above or behind the bit or leans on the side reins, it's often worth trying different equipment.

For instance, you might want to look at the Lungie Bungie, designed by Australian event rider Clayton Fredericks. Many trainers like this because it does not interfere with the horse's lateral flexion and, like the elastic schooling rein, incorporates a certain amount of give.

2.8 The Lungie Bungie does not interfere with lateral flexion and incorporates a certain amount of 'give'.

Stage 3

The final stage in developing your horse on the lunge is to ask him to use his hindquarters and hind legs with more activity and to step under. The best way of doing this is to lunge with two reins – or long-rein on a circle, whichever term you prefer – or to use an EquiAmi or Pessoa training aid. Whatever method you use, vocal aids and, where applicable, correct use of a lunge whip (to guide and encourage the horse, not to chase him) is essential. Some people use the latter two from day one of a rehabilitation programme and there may be occasions when your vet or chartered physiotherapist advises you to do so. However, in most cases, working through stages 1 and 2 and then introducing one of them is more logical, as the right building blocks are in place.

Long-reining

Long-reining, whether on a circle as just described, or on a straight line, can be really beneficial. It gives you an inside and an outside rein, as when riding, so you can ask the horse to bend. Also, when you long-rein on a circle, the feeling of the reins around the horse's hindquarters encourages him to step under more with his hind legs.

Whilst some horses accept long-reins readily, others may be startled when they first feel them – so introduce them carefully, standing at the horse's side and moving them gradually down his neck and body. Most people use ordinary lunge reins, but some trainers prefer to use leather driving reins or ropes because they find this allows more sensitivity. If a horse is heavier on one side than the other – or you know you tend to take a stronger hold with one hand – try using a thinner rein on this side to discourage you from inadvertently allowing an uneven contact.

Although we all ride with two reins, the idea of long-reining seems to make some people nervous. It isn't rocket science and there isn't as much mystique to it as some trainers like to imply. However, there are some ground rules for safety and consistency.

- Always wear gloves and, ideally, a hat.

- If you haven't long-reined before, practise with a horse who knows what it's about.

- Position yourself so you are out of kicking reach.

- Long-reining in a straight line, or driving, is a good way of starting fitness work with a horse who can't be ridden and can also be useful for encouraging a horse to go forward. However, if you are working alone, it must be in safe surroundings. If you want to long-rein on roads or public tracks, you need someone who can walk alongside and if necessary, go to the horse's head.

- Standing slightly to one side gives more control than standing directly behind the horse. If he does spook or take off, it's easier to turn him and you're less likely to give an impromptu imitation of water skiing.

- As with all lungeing and groundwork exercises, your horse should be worked in a simple snaffle. Don't use one that exerts leverage, for example, a three-ring or hanging cheek snaffle, because the length of the reins will increase the pressure capable of being exerted on the horse's mouth.

- Let individual circumstances dictate whether you pass the reins through stirrup irons or roller rings. It's usually safer to do one of the other when you are long-reining on straight lines, but when working on a circle, either leave the reins free or pass just the outside one through the iron or ring. If you do this with the inside rein, you are in danger of locking the bit on the horse's mouth and applying too much pressure. Stirrup irons should be secured to the girth because, if they flap around and bang against the horse's side, he is likely to buck, take off, or both.

If you're still not confident of your dexterity, try the Feeline, developed by trainer Claire Lilley. Each end has a small, static clip and a larger, sliding one.

2.9 *left* Standing slightly to one side whilst long-reining in a straight line gives more control than if you are standing directly behind the horse.

2.10 *below* Stirrup irons should be secured to the girth to prevent them flapping around and startling the horse.

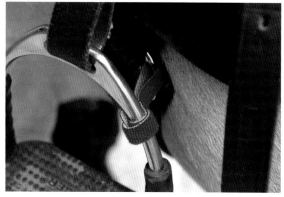

To lunge on the right rein, stand on the nearside with the Feeline coiled in your right hand and fasten the static clip to the nearside bit ring and the sliding one to a ring midway down the roller. Laying the coiled end over the horse's back, move to the offside and take the Feeline over the horse's back. Holding it in your left hand, reverse the clip positions so that the second static clip goes on the roller ring and the second sliding clip on the bit ring (see photo 2.11).

Using the Feeline enables you to hold the reins exactly as when you are riding and many people find it easier to maintain a sensitive 'feel.' When you introduce the Feeline, keep the outside rein over the horse's back, then, as you become confident and if he seems settled, bring it down around his hindquarters so that it rests just above his hocks, and maintain just enough contact to keep it there.

2.11 Those who find it difficult to maintain dexterity when long-reining on a circle may be more comfortable using the Feeline.

Other training aids

The EquiAmi (photo 2.12) and Pessoa lungeing systems look complicated, but are actually quite simple to fit and use. The Pessoa can be used in four positions, according to the horse's stage of training and what you are trying to achieve. The first, or low, position is said to encourage the horse to stretch, but in my experience it is easier to achieve this by using a Chambon. However, once you get to stage 3 of the lungeing programme and want to use a Pessoa, it's sensible to start with this position.

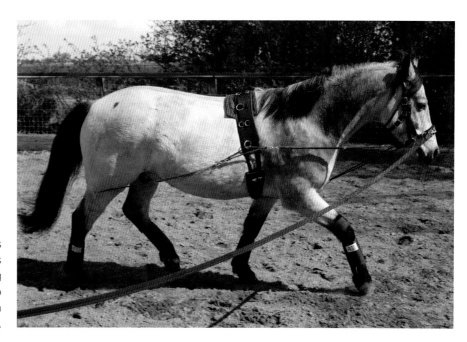

2.12 The EquiAmi is particularly effective as part of a retraining programme for horses who have built up muscle on the underside of the neck.

The second position is said to improve engagement of the hocks and improve muscle development, though strictly speaking, muscle development should happen gradually from stage 1. The third or high position is designed to approximate to the 'on the bit' posture of the ridden horse and is said to help improve the quality of the canter. If used for this purpose, keep canter periods short. The final option is described by the importers as the 'dressage position,' but there are very few horses and trainers for whom it would be suitable.

The EquiAmi is a more recent development and although it looks similar to the Pessoa, in my experience it offers more benefits. The action seems to be more subtle and even horses renowned for being 'stroppy' have accepted it calmly. It is also impossible for a horse to use it to lean on the bit. Whilst the Pessoa is only used for lungeing, the EquiAmi is available in versions for riding, lungeing or both and has been particularly successful when used for retraining ex-racehorses and others who have a build-up of muscle underneath the neck.

Ground poles

Using poles on the ground as part of your lungeing and long-reining sessions is a great way of encouraging your horse to stretch and open out his stride. Just walking him in hand over a pole on the ground means he needs to lower his head and neck, whilst lungeing him over poles placed in a fan shape means you can ask him to lengthen or shorten his stride according to where you direct him.

At World Horse Welfare, simple leading exercises over poles aid assessment and rehabilitation and are ideas that all owners can copy. Walking a serpentine around poles on the ground – an exercise they have nicknamed the slalom – is used to find out whether a horse is stiffer on one side than the other. Walking over and round four poles on the ground is another favourite: if the aim is to encourage the horse to round his back and lift his abdominal muscles, the distances will be shorter than his normal stride length and to free the shoulder, they will be longer.

The box of poles exercise (photos 2.15 and 2.16) is one that can be carried out either on long-reins or under saddle and really encourages the horse to step under with his inside hind leg. Make a square of poles with enough room at each corner for the horse to pass through and approach in various directions, first in walk and then in trot. The idea is to keep the rhythm and bend as you do so – and if you do this whilst long-reining, you'll find it does a lot for your fitness!

Walking and, when appropriate, trotting over poles with alternate ends raised about 15 cm (6 in) from the ground will encourage your horse to use his joints and shoulders and improve his co-ordination. Start with three in a

2.13 and **2.14** Walking a horse in hand over and round poles on the ground is a good way of encouraging him to round his back and lift his abdominal muscles.

line placed flat on the ground and work the horse over them. Next, raise one end of the last pole, then raise the opposite end of the middle pole and finally raise the first pole. You can gradually build up to a line of six poles with alternate raised ends, but as this is hard work for a horse, you must be careful not to overdo it.

2.15 and **2.16** The box of poles exercise encourages the horse to step under with his inside hind leg and, because it contains plenty of variety, also keeps him interested.

2.17 Working a horse over poles with raised ends, either in hand or under saddle, encourages him to flex his joints.

Chapter **Three**

Feeding and environment

THE WAY YOU KEEP and feed your horse has a real impact on the way he looks, performs and behaves, so it's important to get it right. Not only will you be making the most of what he has to offer, you could find that he has more to offer than you realised! In some cases, you could also find that taking a new look at what you feed can save you money and/or help solve problems.

Is his environment horse-friendly or is it designed purely for human convenience? In recent years there has been a school of thought in some sections of the horse world that all horses should live out day and night, all year round – but for some owners, that just isn't possible and there are also horses for whom it doesn't work or would not be suitable. Although it's essential that a horse has sufficient turnout, some seem to prefer being stabled part of the time, so if you're operating a combined system and your horse seems happy and relaxed, don't send yourself on an unnecessary guilt trip.

If you do operate a 24/7 outdoor lifestyle for your horse, check that his environment is correctly maintained. Keeping horses out on well cared for, free-draining land with adequate shelter is a world apart from leaving them out day and night in acres of mud. With changing climates, all year round shelter is essential to give protection against wind, rain and insects.

In some parts of the UK, getting planning consent for field shelters isn't always easy. Mobile shelters can sometimes be the

3.1 Keeping horses on well-maintained grazing, such as this, is very different from leaving them out in acres of mud.

answer as, with these, planning permission is not always needed – though it's important to check with your local authority.

Stable influences

Stable design has a huge influence on a horse's physical and mental well-being. Minimum floor areas are often quoted as 3 x 3 m (10 x 10 ft) for a small pony and 3.7 x 3.7 m (12 x 12 ft) for a horse up to 16 hh – but these really are the minimum sizes and, the bigger the stable, the better off he will be. If you're building your own stables or keep your horse on a DIY livery yard and are offered a bigger box, don't worry about the cost of extra bedding: it will cost a little more to put down a start-up bed, but because your horse has more room to move about, he will be less likely to kick droppings about and his bed will stay cleaner.

Adding an extra window in the back wall of a stable is an easy and relatively cheap way to improve your horse's outlook. This not only increases ventilation, it gives him an extra view, though you need to make sure the back window can be closed if it becomes so windy that he cannot get out of the way of draughts.

If you keep your horse at home and he lives next door to a compatible neighbour, think about having a grille between their stables rather than a solid dividing wall. This enables the horses to see each other and touch noses. If you're on a yard where this isn't possible, installing a special (shatterproof) stable mirror may make your horse happier, as most horses take comfort from their own reflections. This has also been shown to reduce stereotypic behaviour, especially weaving, in many cases.

For many owners, the American barn system of stabling offers the perfect working environment. At one time, some designs perhaps did not offer ideal ventilation, but modern barns are both horse and human friendly, offering a good rate of air exchange. It's also possible to have windows or top doors to the outside at the back, which gives horses more to look at as well as extra ventilation.

Using a large, open-sided barn instead of individual stables can be an option that many horses adapt to happily, though practical and economical considerations mean that straw is the only feasible bedding option. This isn't ideal, as is explained in the next section, but unless your horse eats the

3.2 Installing a grille so that compatible, long-term neighbours can see each other and touch noses makes for a happier environment, but is obviously impossible if there is a rapid changeover of horses and a consequent risk of infections being spread.

straw – which he shouldn't be too tempted to do if he has ad lib forage – the extra ventilation may compensate for having to use it. Two or three compatible horses will live together happily in a barn system, though you need to make sure that there is plenty of forage in different sites to prevent any of them being bullied – and if they have bucket feeds, you usually need to make arrangements for them to be separated whilst they eat.

A breath of fresh air

The most common threat to your horse's health is not infectious disease, but dust and mould spores. Recurrent airway obstruction, or RAO, is the modern and more accurate name for what used to be termed chronic obstructive pulmonary disease, or COPD. We now know that it affects up to 80 per cent of horses, especially those who are stabled all or most of the time.

Of course, not every case is debilitating: in its mildest form, it may produce nothing more than a slight nasal discharge. However, it should never be ignored, because the more your horse's respiratory system comes under threat, the more likely is the emergence of long-term or permanent debilitating effects.

Since guidelines for managing RAO are best practice for *all* horses and ponies and centre on establishing and maintaining an environment that is as free from dust as possible, don't be complacent. The fact that your horse doesn't cough doesn't mean he is not under threat. To minimise the risks, follow the plan below.

• Keep your horse out as much as possible.

• Make sure his stable is well ventilated but also free from draughts. Adding a window at the back of the stable will facilitate air exchange as well as giving him a room with an extra view, but even if there are times when you need to shut this, never shut the top stable door. If you're worried about him getting cold, first remember that horses happily withstand temperatures much lower than humans are comfortable with – what they really hate is a combination of wind and rain. If you're really sure he needs to be warmer, leave the top door open and use an extra or different rug.

• Choose bedding that is as dust-free as possible, perhaps combining it with rubber matting. Some owners like to use rubber matting alone, but although most horses will lie down on it happily, some are reluctant to stale (urinate) because they dislike being splashed – which seems fair enough! Also, with this matting alone, droppings get kicked around more and rugs become dirtier. Using even a small amount of bedding helps prevent this, though many owners prefer to use the same amount as they would put on a concrete floor.

- Be careful how you muck out. Always take your horse out of the stable, as opposed to following the traditional racing stables practice of tying him up inside and mucking out round him. Following the latter practice means that you are throwing dirt and dust into the air and he can't help but breathe it in. For the same reason, don't groom him inside the stable, as you will be sending dust and skin flakes into the air.

- Muck out daily – deep litter systems are deeply unhealthy, as the air is contaminated by ammonia from the build-up of urine and faeces. The exception to this is deep littering with an enzyme product which removes the harmful elements.

- Feed haylage or soaked hay. Soaked hay only offers health benefits whilst it remains wet; as soon as it dries out, dust spores attack the respiratory system again.

3.3 *below left* Taking your horse out of the stable to groom him is far healthier for his – and your – respiratory system than spreading dust and grease by grooming him in his box.

3.4 *below right* Haylage is one of the healthiest forage options for a horse's respiratory system.

- Maintaining a healthy environment for your horse is only beneficial if his neighbours are kept the same way. If the horse next to him is bedded on straw or fed on dry hay, this will also affect his airspace.

- If he has access to a field shelter outdoors, follow the same environmental rules and again, soak hay or feed haylage.

Fat or fit?

Obesity is as great a problem in horses as it is in people. We've all been shocked at the pictures of starving equines taken in by welfare organisations such as World Horse Welfare, but overfeeding can be just as damaging as underfeeding. And whilst there have been huge advances in equine nutrition over the past few years, it's important to be realistic in your expectations.

Just as it's tempting to believe that expensive skin creams can make you look ten years younger (an admittedly sexist comparison, but one that male readers will hopefully forgive) so you may assume that this feed or that supplement will make your horse jump higher, go faster or piaffe with more power. Sadly, it doesn't work that way and you may find that what you put in one end literally comes out the other.

Having said that, whilst feed companies are obviously in business to make money, they are only as good as their reputations. Most of the big names have helplines and advisers who will give free advice based on their own products and seem to take the attitude that their job is to help you do the best for your horse, not to persuade you to buy as many feeds and supplements as possible.

Eating like a horse

It's no coincidence that someone who enjoys his or her food is often said to 'eat like a horse'. When horses are turned out, or given ad lib forage, eating is what they do most of. However, this is natural behaviour rather than greed: the horse is a grazing animal with a digestive system designed to take in a continuous trickle of forage, not to survive on two to four bucket meals a day plus a couple of haynets every 24 hours.

As a prey animal, he is also meant to eat on the move. By confining him for long periods and reducing grazing time, we impose psychological stress and can easily end up with a horse who is compromised mentally and physically. Whilst it isn't always possible or practical to keep a horse out all the time, it's important to keep him in a way that mimics natural behaviour and if he is the sort who 'lives on fresh air', or is prone to laminitis, use strategies such as strip grazing to minimise the risks, as explained later in this chapter.

Has your grazing been established for horses, or is it more suited to cattle? There are significant differences between these types of pasture, that reflect the different requirements and digestive systems of the two species. If your horse is munching his way through a sward formulated to boost milk or meat yields, you're heading for problems and need to find grazing that is less dense in nutrients. Obviously, it should still be good quality and free from harmful weeds. If a total change of grazing is impossible, you need to use other strategies, such as strip grazing. This means fencing off an area that has already been grazed down – but not over-grazed – either by horses who are not susceptible to threats from rich grazing, or by sheep. If you know your horse or pony is susceptible to laminitis, you may also need to keep him off grazing when fructans – water-soluble carbohydrates found in grass – are not at high levels.

The safest period is thought to be from dusk until dawn. However, when grass has frost on it, fructan levels shoot up, so try not to turn out in these conditions. There has also been a re-think on the old advice of turning out animals susceptible to laminitis on bare paddocks with sparse grass growing through, since the resulting 'stressed' grass is also high in fructans. If an over-grazed area is all that is available, ask your vet's advice on whether putting out clean hay with a low nutritional value is a viable strategy; alternatively, consider whether you can use an arena or large crew yard and put out hay at different points to provide a choice of eating places.

If in doubt, ask your vet's advice. We now know that there are many possible causes of laminitis, but it's important to minimise the known risks, to prevent animals at risk become overweight – advice that, in any case, applies to all equines – and to feed a high-fibre diet.

How much?

There is an old saying that 'The eye of the master makes the horse fat.' In today's parlance, that can be translated into the advice that if you keep a critical eye on your horse's condition by carrying out regular condition scoring, you'll ensure that he doesn't become too fat or too thin. However, whilst 'feeding by eye' is an essential skill, so is having a practical basis as a foundation for this.

The first step is to find out how much your horse weighs which, as well as helping you formulate his basic diet, will ensure that you administer the correct dosage of wormer. For most owners, the only practical way of doing this is to use a weigh tape once a month; follow the manufacturer's instructions carefully for placing it round your horse or you won't get reliable readings. The most accurate way of measuring weight is to use a weighbridge, but these are usually only available at veterinary practices and on some racing yards. If you take your horse to your vet's practice for routine preventive care, it's worth putting him on a weighbridge to get an accurate benchmark figure, which you can then compare with your weigh tape reading. However, using a weigh tape alone will still make you aware of minor weight gain or loss that you might not spot simply through observation, particularly when you see your horse every day. Having said that, you don't want to become a weight obsessive by proxy!

Knowing your horse's weight makes it easier to formulate quantities of feed, supplements and medications. The general advice is that, to maintain his present condition, he needs to consume 2–2.5 per cent of his weight in feed each day, but if he needs to lose weight, this should fall to 1.5–2 per cent. Feeding severely underweight horses must be done with expert advice; many will lack appetite and even if they don't, you can cause digestive problems, including colic, by overloading the digestive system.

Of course, it isn't just a case of *how much* you feed your horse – *what* you feed also has to be decided. The bottom line in every case is that forage should make up the greatest part of the diet, both to keep your horse's digestive system functioning properly and to keep him happy. Horses need to chew, both psychologically and physiologically. Physiologically, chewing produces saliva, which acts as a buffer against stomach acid, and the fact that they have some forage to chew on means that there is something for the acid to act upon. When they don't have the opportunity to chew adequately, they are more likely to get problems such as gastric ulcers.

3.5 Using a weigh tape once a month will make you aware of fluctuations in your horse's weight.

Most horses and ponies who would be categorised as Riding Club/Pony Club animals function and perform well on a diet in which good quality forage, plus a broad-spectrum vitamin and mineral supplement, makes up 80–100 per cent of their intake.

Grass has a high water content and will provide between half and all of a horse's forage needs, depending on how long he is turned out for. If grass is sparse and/or lacking in feed value, you will need to provide hay or haylage of a feed value appropriate to your horse's needs – and also to any problems he might have, such as susceptibility to laminitis or being overweight – in the field as well as in the stable. If you are feeding a good doer or an animal at risk of laminitis, this must be taken into account. The emphasis is on quality, as there is a world of difference between good-quality, correctly stored hay, or haylage, and hay that is so old it has lost most of its nutritional value and/or is dusty.

Haylage is now available in different grades to suit different nutritional needs, so get advice from a nutritionist and/or specialist grower – you don't want to feed high-energy haylage to a fatty and you also need to take into account the moisture content. Because haylage is bagged or wrapped when the cut grass is semi-wilted, it always has a higher moisture content and is lower in fibre than hay, which is baled when the grass is dry. As a rule of thumb, you will therefore need to feed at least as much haylage by weight as you would dry hay.

Horses in really hard work – and that means examples such as racehorses in full training and advanced event and endurance horses in peak fitness, not a horse who hacks or schools for an hour every day and competes at weekends – may need up to 50 per cent of their diet as hard feed, but the forage ration should never go below half of the total diet. There are, of course, a multitude of scenarios between these examples, which is where common sense and, where appropriate, professional advice come in.

When your horse really needs extra fuel in the form of hard feed, choose one appropriate to his type and his *current* workload, not what you *intend* him to do or *hope* he will become. Feeding a competition mix won't turn him into a competition horse – and there are plenty of horses competing at top level in eventing and other disciplines on feeds marketed for all-rounders. Make the most of the scientific advances in nutrition, but don't be seduced by marketing. For instance, there are now feeds that make it much easier to keep older horses healthy, but there are also plenty of 'guilt traps' for owners to fall into. Before you buy this or that supplement, be honest about whether he really needs it.

It isn't just *what* you feed that affects your horse's well-being, it's the way you feed it. Try to reproduce the horse's grazing stance whenever possible by feeding from the ground. This allows the horse to maintain a natural grinding pattern on his teeth and also helps avoid a build-up of muscle underneath the neck.

Feeding for weight loss

In the UK there are far more overweight horses and ponies than there are underweight ones. Don't believe the myth that you can 'turn fat into muscle' – it's a nonsensical physical impossibility, but unfortunately an idea that tempts some owners to overfeed young horses. In doing so, they put them at risk of contracting laminitis and from the strain imposed by excess weight on immature joints trying to support it.

Feeding a horse or pony who needs to lose weight isn't as easy as you might think. It isn't simply a case of cutting down on food, because if you do that, you restrict the time a horse needs to spend chewing. Also, because the equine digestive system needs to be kept working, you increase the risk of digestive problems and of a metabolic condition called hyperlipidaemia. The best way round these problems is to maintain the horse on low-energy but still good-quality forage: ideally, late-cut hay that has been soaked for 12 hours.

At one time, it was thought that hay should always be soaked overnight to minimise respiratory problems. Nutritionists now advise soaking for shorter periods so that it is thoroughly wetted, but nutrients are not leached out. If you want to cut calories, it therefore makes sense to soak hay for 12 hours to reduce its energy value. A broad-spectrum vitamin and mineral supplement mixed with a handful of low-energy chaff will take care of missing nutrients – and if you want to keep a horse happy when others are being fed, offer sliced carrots, apples or swedes in his manger.

You will probably need to restrict his grazing, either by strip grazing, as explained earlier, or by using a grazing muzzle.

Feeding for weight gain

If a horse needs to gain weight, first ask your vet to make a dental check and organise a faecal egg count. As your vet will explain, egg counts identify egg-laying adult parasites, not those who are developing, migrating or in encysted stages – and they don't identify tapeworms, though a blood test which will do so is available through your vet. However, egg counts offer a good snapshot of an animal's current parasite burden.

The best way to put weight on a healthy horse with a normal appetite is to feed forage that has a higher energy value, or to replace part of his forage ration with dried chopped grass or alfalfa. Other strategies include adding soaked sugar beet pulp or shreds to his diet, as this has an energy level similar to that of a 'medium' level compound feed, but is also high in fibre. Soya or vegetable oil also add calories and are said to help promote a healthy coat.

You can also try feeding a cube or mix formulated to increase his calorie intake without increasing the amount of starch in his diet beyond acceptable levels: ask your feed company nutritionist for advice.

Alternatively, give more of his current feed. However, as horses are designed to be 'trickle feeders' rather than to consume relatively large amounts in one go, feed little and often rather than piling the extra into a couple of large feeds. Ensure that each manger feed – including chaff and other extras – does not weigh more than 0.4 kg per 100 kg (14 oz per 220 lb) body weight. For example, the maximum weight of a meal for a 350 kg (770 lb) pony would be 1.4 kg (3 lb), and for a 500 kg (1,100 lb) horse, the maximum weight would be 2 kg (4 lb 6 oz).

Balancers

Feed balancers have become increasingly popular over the past few years, though they are perhaps not the universal answer some marketing campaigns would suggest. Basically, they are either compound feeds in a concentrated version, or formulated to balance out deficiencies in straight cereals for owners who prefer to feed them. The advantage of the concentrated compound versions is that they allow you to make sure your horse receives all the nutrients and micronutrients he needs and, because they are fed in small quantities – usually around 500 g (just over 1 lb) per day – they are relatively low in calories when used to complement a forage-only diet.

Conversely, they can also be used to top-up a compound feed to add extra nutrients, though if you feel you need to do this, get expert advice to avoid the risk of micronutrient overload. The downside of balancers is that most are relatively expensive.

Feed supplements

We all want to do the best for our horses, so it's easy to assume that every horse needs one or more of the huge range of supplements – or, as they should technically be called, complementary feeding stuffs – available. Whilst nutritional support can be valuable in some cases, there are many owners who are simply feeding their horses to produce very expensive manure. You also need to remember that if the basics of the diet aren't right, a supplement isn't going to provide a quick fix.

However, most horses do not get enough of a vital and inexpensive item in their diet: simple salt. This applies particularly to animals on a high-forage diet, as forage is low in sodium, which is one of the two components of common salt. One way of getting round this is to give free access to a salt lick, but some horses become rather over-enthusiastic about this and in these cases, it's safer to add a total of two tablespoons daily in the feed.

In many cases, a broad-spectrum vitamin and mineral supplement will make good any deficiencies in these substances. The following scenarios are good examples:

- If a horse is getting less than the manufacturer's recommended amount of a compound feed or mix. This applies in many cases, as recommended amounts are often far too high and would result in a horse becoming overweight. Feed your supplement at half the recommended rate.

- When the diet is based wholly or mainly on forage (though, at the same time, take credit for feeding your horse as nature intended!). This time, add the broad-spectrum supplement at the recommended rate for his weight.

- If soil – and therefore grazing – is known to be deficient in particular nutrients. This is by no means uncommon, although the specific deficiency will vary from area to area. For instance, in parts of East Anglia, soil is low in magnesium. You can test for deficiencies by having soil analysis carried out. There are DIY kits available, but these are intended mainly for gardens. For anything over 0.4 hectare (1 acre), it's best to get a specialist contractor with knowledge of horses' nutritional needs to do the analysis for you.

- When you feed straight cereals rather than compound feeds. As a practice, this isn't generally recommended. When you buy a compound feed, you also buy the assurance that every bag meets the same nutritional requirements. With straight cereals, nutrients vary from batch to batch.

Problems and supplements

If your horse has a physical or behavioural problem, always start by getting veterinary advice where necessary and looking at your overall management. If an older horse seems stiff, he may well be showing signs of arthritis – but you need a clinical diagnosis, and the only person who can provide that is a vet.

Feeding a supplement to provide 'joint support' may well be helpful if arthritis is indeed the problem, but if your horse is showing signs of mild exertional rhabdomyolysis (tying up), or a badly fitting saddle is causing discomfort, you won't be helping him. Trying to diagnose and treat your horse without veterinary advice is tantamount to neglect.

Similarly, whilst some behavioural problems may improve with nutritional support, start by looking at the big picture. Is your horse excitable or grumpy because he doesn't get turned out enough, or because he doesn't get enough exercise, or because he's getting too much hard feed? Is he coughing because you are not maintaining a dust-free management system?

Last but not least, is it a partnership problem rather than a behavioural one? If your horse is naturally forward going and reactive and you're a slightly nervous rider, are you tensing up, perhaps taking a stronger contact with his mouth than he is happy with and thus causing a vicious circle?

If you can honestly say that your basic care and management programme is sound, nutritional support might be the final piece in the jigsaw. However, don't fall into the trap of thinking that because a supplement is described as 'natural' or 'herbal,' it is harmless. Many herbs have contra-indications; for example devil's claw stimulates the uterine muscles in mares and also the digestive system, so should not be given to pregnant mares or animals with stomach ulcers.

By the same token, don't combine supplements or use more than the recommended amounts without getting qualified advice, or you could cause problems. If your horse is on medication from your vet, ask his or her advice before adding a supplement in case this could react adversely or interfere with the prescribed medicine.

You also need to be careful if you compete, as some substances (herbal or otherwise) are forbidden under the rules of the various disciplines.

Having made these points, let's look at some types of supplement available, and how they may help with certain conditions.

Joint supplements

There is huge anecdotal evidence for the efficacy of some supplements in helping to support joint function. As with most equine research, the majority of scientific evidence comes from the field of human medicine. Some experts believe this can muddy the waters – for a start, all dosage rates have to be extrapolated from those for people.

Whilst there is general acceptance that glucosamine is beneficial to horses, opinions vary on whether chondroitin sulphate, with which it is often paired, can help. Glucosamine occurs naturally in the horse, but studies have shown that chondroitin sulphate cannot be absorbed by the horse when given orally.

Methyl suphonyl methane (MSM), a bio-available source of sulphur, is another popular 'nutraceutical'. MSM is present in small quantities in many plants, including grasses, but extra supplementation may be needed if the aim is to try to improve joint health. Other 'natural' nutritional aids said to help include cider apple vinegar, devil's claw and Omega-3 and Omega-6 oils.

Hoof supplements

The best aids to healthy hooves are a balanced diet and good farriery. However, research now shows that some nutrients are especially useful to some horses: unfortunately, you can supply them but you can't guarantee that your horse will be able to absorb them. Anecdotal evidence suggests that the following may help:

Biotin – this is a B-vitamin which helps maintain a correct water balance, and therefore good quality hoof horn. General advice is that it should be fed in conjunction with methionine and zinc.

Magnesium – essential for healthy hoof growth. There is also anecdotal evidence that adequate levels of magnesium may help prevent or lessen sole sensitivity.

Methionine – a 'building block' for healthy connective tissue.

Zinc – essential for the formation of healthy keratin, present in the outer layers of horn and skin.

Copper, vitamin C and essential fatty acids are also important for healthy hooves and if your horse's diet is deficient in these, you may need to supplement them.

Probiotics and prebiotics

These both help maintain a healthy balance of microorganisms in the horse's digestive system, but work in different ways. The microorganisms, which include bacteria and forms of yeast, break down fibre in the hindgut so that the nutrients from it can be absorbed.

In basic terms, a probiotic is a live product that can colonise the gut. It should be used in the short term, in situations where bacteria need to be replaced: for instance, as extreme examples it would be beneficial if a horse has had laminitis or colic surgery. A prebiotic is a feed component that cannot be digested by the horse's gut enzymes and is therefore available to the gut microorganisms, and can thus help to maintain them at healthy levels. This can help avoid digestive disturbance at times when the system is stressed so they might, for example, be helpful to a horse who gets worried by travelling. Prebiotics are sometimes included in feeds though, in general, are fed over a shorter period than probiotics. However, some people use one all the time because they say that this is the only way they can ensure that their horse has droppings of a 'normal' consistency. This practice won't do any harm but veterinary advice should be sought to try to find out the underlying cause of the problem. You can feed a prebiotic for a longer period because you're only feeding the bacteria that are already there; you're not adding to them.

Calmers

Products formulated to promote calmness, commonly known as calmers, form one of the biggest-selling sectors of the supplements market and cause more controversy than any other feed additives. There is huge anecdotal evidence that some have a beneficial effect in some cases, though cynics argue that this may be only because the rider thinks they will work and relaxes accordingly. Perhaps an even more cynical view is to suggest that if it works, who cares?

My own experience is that magnesium-based supplements can help with young or nervous animals, especially whilst they are being backed or are settling into a new home. Whilst fully accepting that all horses take and should be allowed time to relax in a new environment, I also live in an area where the soil is so deficient in magnesium that dairy farmers have to provide it for their cows to prevent them getting hypomagnesaemia, an often fatal condition commonly known as grass staggers. If it seems likely that your horse might benefit from magnesium supplementation, get expert advice from your vet or a qualified nutritionist on the safest and most effective form; some authorities believe that this is magnesium oxide.

Supplements to treat stereotypic behaviour

In the past few years, antacid products have been developed that are said to reduce or even eliminate crib-biting in some horses. However, horses who demonstrate stereotypic behaviour – weaving, crib-biting or wind-sucking – often stop, or at least reduce such behaviour, when given more turnout and/or forage, so look to your management regime first. Also, as mentioned earlier in this chapter, stable mirrors are successful in reducing this behaviour in some cases.

Supplementary feeding for a healthy coat

A healthy horse on a balanced diet should have a healthy coat and if you want to put a shine on it, what you put on the inside is as important as what you do to the outside. Although some marketed supplements are claimed to support the growth of a healthy coat, research has shown that linseed oil and soya oil are most easily absorbed by the horse's digestive system and should therefore benefit the skin, hair and hoof quality. However, oils are dense in calories, so you wouldn't want to feed them to a horse who needs to lose weight.

Food for thought

This chapter is not intended to be an in-depth guide on how and what to feed your horse; there are plenty of specialist titles that deal with nothing else and plenty of information available from feed companies. However, to make the most of your horse, you need to make sure you follow the best principles. Some of the general points below may help you to take a look at your horse's diet and the choices you make and perhaps make some improvements. At the very least, you may save money.

- Check your horse's weight by using a weigh tape each month and at the same time, carry out a condition score.

- Remember the importance of dental care and worming measures.

- Never underestimate the importance of forage in your horse's diet – and look after it. Maintaining grazing and storing hay so that it remains dry and clean will benefit your horse and your pocket.

- Keep your horse hydrated – one of the golden rules of feeding is to ensure that clean, fresh water is available at all times. If he is working hard, get advice from your vet or feed company nutritionist on whether he would benefit from electrolytes.

3.6 Regular dental care is an essential part of your horse's overall health and well-being and will also ensure that he gets maximum value from his feed.

- Feed by weight, not by volume. You don't have to weigh every feed, every day, but check once a week or so that you're not gradually over- or under-feeding.

- If you change from one brand of feed to another, do so gradually over several days to avoid disturbing your horse's digestive system.

- If you cut down his work, cut down his hard feed. If you plan to increase his work, do this *before* increasing his feed.

- Feed for what he is and what he's doing, not what you aim to do or what you hope he will turn into.

Chapter **Four**

Tack

THE TACK YOU USE AFFECTS your horse's comfort, the ease and effectiveness with which you communicate with him and even his soundness. For instance, a badly fitting saddle can quickly cause muscle damage and although there is no such thing as a magic bit that makes every horse go beautifully, finding one which suits your horse's mouth conformation and stage of training can have a marked effect.

On a less important note – but still a factor to take into account if you want to present your horse looking his best – tack can improve or detract from the overall picture you present. In particular, the right bridle can make a plain head look workmanlike and handsome.

You need to think about the tack you are using, and why. Do you use an eggbutt or a loose-ring snaffle because that's what your horse was ridden in when you bought him? If he goes nicely in it, there is no reason to change it, but if you aren't happy with your communication, it's a piece in the overall jigsaw that should be looked at.

What sort of noseband do you use? Are you using one which fastens above and below the bit, such as a Flash, out of habit and if so, what happens if you remove the strap or change your noseband for a plain cavesson?

Do you always use a martingale? If so, do you need it – especially when schooling on the flat, when it may give a false impression of your horse's way of going?

What about training aids? Do you have a tack room full of draw reins and other devices, always hoping to find the one thing that will make your horse magically go on the bit? Or are you fervently 'anti-gadget'? Both approaches can turn out to be negative, as is discussed later in this chapter.

You also need to look at how your tack affects your riding. This applies particularly to saddles (see Fitting the Rider, later this chapter), which need to suit the conformation of the rider as well as the horse and to be of an appropriate design for the horse's job and the rider's level of ability. In some cases, tack can also help to *minimise* faults and keep your horse comfortable. For instance, if a rider has unsteady hands, using a bit which remains relatively fixed in the horse's mouth minimises the effects of unwanted movement, as does using a *correctly fitted* running martingale.

In the hot seat

Although saddle fitting and alteration are specialist jobs, every rider needs to know how to recognise a well-fitting saddle and how to spot when professional advice is needed. Horses change shape when they gain or lose weight and build or lose muscle, so a saddle which fits perfectly in summer or when a horse is just backed will often need altering a few months – or even a few weeks – later.

Many riders buy saddles without taking professional advice, especially when second-hand 'bargains' are seen to be had on internet auction sites or mail order. But though the price you pay buying from an auction or advert may be lower than when buying a second-hand saddle from a qualified saddler, it may not be cheaper in the long run. The expertise required to check, repair if necessary and make any alterations needed before fitting it to your horse usually pays dividends.

There is a difference between shops that act simply as retailers and saddlers with expertise in fitting and alteration. In the UK, one of the easiest ways to find a good fitter is to look for someone with the Society of Master Saddlers' fitting qualification (though that does not necessarily mean that a saddler who does not hold it is not capable). In other countries, it may be more difficult to find someone with a recognised qualification, though local reputation should be a guideline – and there are also fitters with the UK qualification who travel throughout Europe and America.

You may be tempted to think that there are ways round the fitting problem by using a treeless saddle or one which has the Flair airbag system installed. However, there is no such thing as a saddle which fits every horse; there are plenty of professional riders who swear that this is the case, but the real scenario is that their horses are of a similar stamp and shape.

Although I have had nothing but good results from using the Flair system, not everyone likes it. Although it seems to give more flexibility than standard flocking, it still needs to be adjusted correctly to start with and when the horse changes shape.

The pros and cons of treeless saddles are open to debate and much depends on how horse and rider react to a particular design. If this is your preferred option, look for one that has given good results under pressure testing analysis and get help from someone who knows how to use pads, numnahs or shims, when appropriate.

Again, treeless saddles suit some horses and/or riders but not others. In my experience, the best designs manage to incorporate a twist or waist in the seat and so avoid you feeling as if you are sitting on a table.

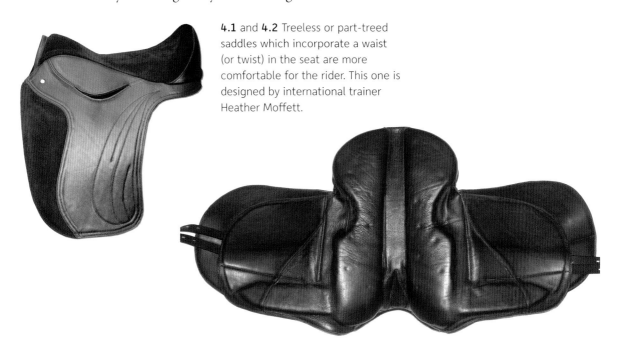

4.1 and **4.2** Treeless or part-treed saddles which incorporate a waist (or twist) in the seat are more comfortable for the rider. This one is designed by international trainer Heather Moffett.

People often assume that damage to a treed saddle is easy to spot, but that isn't always the case. One of the things most potentially damaging to a horse's back is a broken tree, but this isn't always dramatically obvious. Checks to see whether a saddle needs stripping down and examining are outlined in the next section, but even so, the possibility of a hairline fracture might only be picked up by an expert.

Having said that, there are two checks which may give you an idea of whether or not there are potential problems in a saddle with a standard tree:

1. Place the saddle on a flat surface, seat upwards. Put one hand on each point pocket and press hard. If you hear creaks or grinding noises, or the points give more than seems normal, get it checked.

4.3 *above* To get an idea of whether a saddle tree is sound, first place the saddle on a flat surface and press down on the point pockets.

4.4 *right* Next, hold the saddle with the pommel against your stomach and pull the cantle towards you.

2. Now hold the saddle with the pommel pressed into your stomach and pull the cantle towards you. Again, listen out for excessive noises. If the saddle has a spring tree, it will naturally have more give than a rigid one, but it still should not resemble a bendy toy.

When you look at the saddle from above, it should not appear twisted and there should not be excessive creasing of the seat. Either should be treated as warning signs.

Check that the stitching which holds the panel in place is secure; if it is broken or coming loose, the panel will shift. With standard flocking, run your fingers lightly over the panel to feel for lumps or hollows, both signs that the saddle needs the flocking adjusting. Look, also, to see if the panel is symmetrical. If one side is different from the other, this may have been done to take into account a particular horse's asymmetrical shape and, if done by an expert, this can contribute to a good fit *for that horse*. A new saddle should start off with a symmetrical panel and whether you are buying a new or second-hand saddle, you need to get it checked and if necessary, adjusted to fit you and your horse by a specialist saddler.

The stitching that holds the girth straps in place is also vulnerable to wear and tear, so make sure it is in good condition. Whenever you check stitching on tack, do it by feel as well as by eye – give a good tug! It contributes to supporting your weight so any weakness or breakage must be repaired at once.

It's sensible to carry out thorough soundness checks every few weeks – tie this in with checking your saddle fit, as explained below. If you drop your saddle, or a horse rolls whilst tacked up, get it checked before using it again.

Fit for purpose

A good definition of a well-fitting saddle is that it fits the profile of the horse's back, does not interfere with his movement and distributes the rider's weight over as wide an area as possible. It must also enable and encourage the rider to sit comfortably and correctly for the appropriate discipline and suit individual rider conformation. The horse must come first, but don't ignore your own requirements – if you're out of balance, your weight will be distributed unevenly, the way you apply the aids will be affected and in turn, your horse's comfort and way of going will be compromised.

Once you know your saddle is a good fit, you need to check it regularly so that you know when you may need professional help again. You should check it from the ground and with a rider on board – which means getting a helper to assess it whilst you ride, or asking someone of similar weight and shape to ride your horse whilst you take a look. It helps if the person looking at what's going on has some practical knowledge of horses, but it is equally important that he or she is observant; unfortunately, the two don't always go together!

Are you sure your saddle is in the right place? It may seem easy enough to put it on and girth it up – but as any saddler will tell you, a lot of riders place their saddles too far forward. As a horse moves, his shoulder-blades rotate backwards in turn and if the saddle is too far forward, it will interfere with his movement and make him uncomfortable. When the saddle is in place and girthed up, there should be a hand's width between it and the point of the shoulder-blade.

The starting point for fitting a treed saddle is that the tree must be the correct width and profile. If the tree is too narrow, it will pinch on either side of and below the withers. One that is too wide can also cause problems, pressing below and even on top of the withers. The easiest way to measure the profile of your horse's withers is to use a drawing tool called a Flexicurve, available from most art shops. Place it over the horse a hand's width behind the point of the shoulder-blade and mould it to the horse, then lay it on a sheet of paper and draw round the inside.

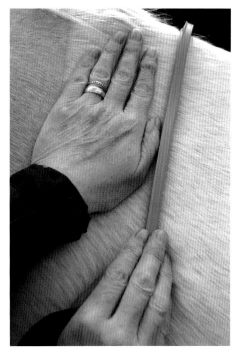

4.5 Use a Flexicurve to measure the profile of your horse's withers.

The other thing to take into account is the shape of the horse's back. Some manufacturers have done a lot of research into this and use trees to follow the shape of common profiles, such as those of flat-backed cobs or horses with high withers. Unfortunately, there are still saddles on sale built on banana-shaped trees, which some riders may be tempted to use in the hope that they will provide a deep, secure seat. The reality is that they only fit horses with dipped backs and, if used on others, will cause pressure points because of the limited bearing surface. When you get a pressure point, the blood supply to the area is restricted or even cut of; in the long term, this can cause muscle wastage and even permanent damage.

4.6 When a saddle is girthed up, the lowest part of the seat should be in the centre.

When the saddle is girthed up, the lowest point of the seat should be in the centre. If not, the rider will be tipped forwards or back and will be struggling to maintain balance. A skilled saddler can alter the saddle's balance by altering the flocking, but if you're fighting your saddle, you're making your life difficult and your horse uncomfortable.

The only way to check saddle fit is with a rider on board. As a matter of course, use a mounting block or take a leg-up whenever possible, rather than mounting from the ground. Although we all have to get on from the ground at times, if you do this every time it inevitably puts strain on the horse's back and the saddle tree.

Next time you are at a competition, notice how many people mount from the ground, grabbing hold of the cantle to pull themselves up and, in doing so, pulling the saddle over to the left. They then stand in their stirrups and push down on the right iron to level it up, which does neither the horse nor the saddle any good.

When the rider is on board, you want to see the following:

- That the saddle is level from front to back and the rider is balanced centrally.

- The panel should be in contact with, but not digging into, the horse. Run your hand down the front of the panel on either side of the withers, then under the rider's thigh and behind it.

- From behind, the saddle should sit centrally. If it sits to one side, is it the saddle – or does the rider have uneven stirrup leathers, or put more weight in one stirrup than the other? Few riders distribute their weight evenly, which is why it's a good idea to switch your stirrup leathers from side to side each time you ride, or use non-stretch leathers.

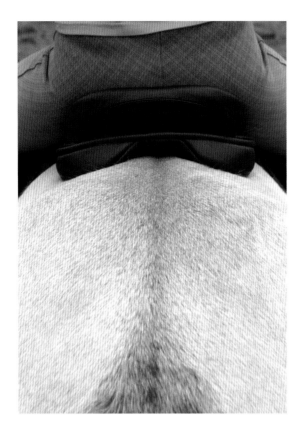

4.7 Seen from behind, the saddle should sit centrally.

- Also from behind, you want to see that the gullet is clear of the horse's back all the way along.

- There should be adequate clearance at the pommel and cantle. It's often stipulated that there should be a space equivalent to the width of three fingers between the pommel and the withers, and the cantle and the back, but this may not always be strictly necessary: it depends on the design of the saddle and the job the horse is doing.

In general, jumping calls for greater clearance than dressage or hacking. This begs the question of whether close-contact saddles, which often a have latex or foam panel said to mould to the horse, but which may offer little scope for adjustment, are a feasible option. Again, take a knowledgeable saddle fitter's advice.

Having made a stationary check of all these points, as long as there are no major problems, horse and rider can now be assessed on the move. For this to be worthwhile, you need to know how the horse moves when he doesn't have a rider's weight on his back, so it's worth watching him on the lunge to get your eye in.

Does he move as freely when ridden on a loose rein as he does on the lunge, or are there signs that something isn't right? If he shortens his stride, goes in a hollow outline or swishes his tail, you need to find out what prompts the change.

Any saddle will move slightly as the horse moves, but you don't want to see it rock noticeably, either from side to side or backwards and forwards. Nor do you want to see the back flipping up and down.

If you're at all worried, get your saddle checked. However, if your horse shows signs of resistance but you can't see any indication that the saddle is to blame, don't automatically assume it's still the root cause. Get it checked as part of an overall investigation, but be prepared to look in other directions, starting by asking your vet to assess your horse.

Fitting the rider

The horse must always be given priority when fitting a saddle, but you have to think about your own needs, too – not just because of your comfort, but because if you are uncomfortable or out of balance, you can't ride correctly or effectively and this will have an adverse affect on your horse. This doesn't mean that a saddle designed for a particular top rider will automatically help you, or that one favoured by your instructor will be the best choice for you and your horse, but there should still be plenty of scope to make sure you're suited.

Does your saddle suit the work you and your horse are doing? Even if you've settled on a general-purpose or specialist design, such as a dressage or showing saddle, there are things to take into account.

If you're a rider who likes to do a bit of everything, a general-purpose saddle is the sensible choice. But as some models are more forward-cut than others, you need to think about your priorities. If you tend to concentrate on schooling on the flat and dressage competitions, with hacking and a bit of jumping to vary your routine, you'll be happier with a slightly straighter-cut design. Some of these are marketed as VSD, which most saddlers now translate as 'very slightly dressage'. On the other hand, riders who like to do plenty of jumping and think that any hack that doesn't incorporate a good canter or two is boring need a saddle that enables them to shorten their stirrup leathers between two and four holes and be able to stay in a balanced, comfortable position without their knees hanging over the edge of the saddle flaps. They will usually be better suited by a general-purpose saddle with a more forward cut.

If your passions are schooling and competing in dressage, you'll inevitably decide to buy a specialised dressage design. There are many lovely saddles on the market, but make sure you choose one that doesn't require a longer leg position than you're currently able to adopt. The one shown in photo 4.8 is popular with many riders, particularly those competing up to Novice/Elementary level at unaffiliated or affiliated competitions because it encourages a correct leg position but doesn't put you out of balance if you take your stirrup leathers up a hole, which can sometimes be useful when hacking or riding an inexperienced or fresh horse – or one who is both.

There are ways to get the best of all worlds. One is to buy a saddle that offers you different options via movable components; the most successful of these is probably the WOW saddle. The other is to buy two saddles that cover all the options you need – for instance, a general-purpose saddle and a dressage model – perhaps keeping down costs by looking at second-hand or synthetic designs. Some of the latest synthetic saddles are well designed, well made and aesthetically attractive and a good synthetic may actually be better than a poor-quality leather saddle.

If you're a showing enthusiast, don't get too carried away by the premise that a saddle has to show off your horse's conformation to best advantage, even if this means it has no knee rolls, a flat seat and encourages a riding position akin to sitting on a loo seat with your legs stuck out in front of you to try to gain some security. There are now modern showing saddles which satisfy aesthetic considerations as well as allowing for rider comfort and security – though there are also still some very rider-unfriendly designs to be seen.

Whatever design you opt for, check that the stirrup bars are set in the appropriate place for that saddle and your purposes. On some saddles, they are set too far forward, so you have to draw back your legs to keep them in a correct position, which in turn, affects your balance and weight distribution. If you don't make an attempt to sit correctly, you'll end up adopting a chair seat, with your legs stuck out in front. More manufacturers are now aware of this, but there are still saddles where the placement is incorrect.

The size of the saddle seat is another important factor. If it's too small, you'll feel like an adult squashed into a child's chair and will be totally uncomfortable, and if it's too big, you may feel as if you're sliding around. There are exceptions to the latter point: some riders prefer a slightly larger

4.8 A dressage saddle should encourage a correct leg position without forcing you to ride with longer stirrup leathers than you're currently able to adopt.

seat when riding cross-country, as it gives them more flexibility to adjust their position when riding over drop fences. However, if you have a generously sized backside and ride a horse with a relatively short back, or a pony, you may have to compromise to ensure that there is no risk of the saddle's weight-bearing area extending too far back. The standard way of measuring seat size on an English saddle is to measure from one front stud, diagonally across the seat to the centre of the cantle (see photo 4.9). On a Western saddle, the measurement goes in a straight line across the seat from the centre of the pommel to the centre of the cantle.

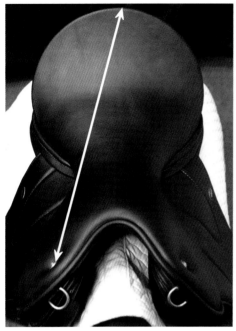

4.9 The traditional way of measuring the seat size of an English saddle is from one front stud, diagonally across to the centre of the cantle.

As well as helping you decide on the correct seat size, a good saddler and fitter will be able to make sure that the length of the flaps and the position of any knee and thigh rolls or blocks complement your build. We aren't all made in the same proportions: some people are relatively long or short from thigh to knee, or from knee to ankle. Customising saddle proportions and layout can make a big difference.

Another anatomical difference to think about is the obvious difference between men and women! Women in particular sometimes find that a particular design of saddle can bring tears to their eyes; an experienced saddle fitter will have come across this problem before, so don't feel embarrassed about mentioning it, as there is bound to be a different saddle that will suit.

Make sure that you try a saddle thoroughly before buying it, especially if it's different from the one you've been used to. For instance, it takes a little time to get used to riding in your first dressage saddle and some people take a while to get used to riding in a treeless or part-treed saddle.

Saddle accessories

The accessories you use with your saddle – numnahs, stirrups and girths – also need consideration.

Most riders like to use a numnah or saddle pad as a matter of course, sometimes because they think the horse will be more comfortable, or simply to keep the underside of the saddle clean. There may also be times when a saddle fitter will suggest using a particular type of pad to help balance a saddle, particularly close-contact designs.

However, make sure that whatever you use contributes towards a good fit rather than compromising it. A thick numnah may have an adverse effect –

you may be asking your horse to do the equivalent of wearing three pairs of socks inside what was originally a well-fitting pair of shoes.

Having said that, there are times when the right numnah or pad can be the final link in solving a problem. Numnahs and saddle cloths with built-in grip pads can be a real help with horses who have low withers and round barrels, and some horses go better with, say, a sheepskin numnah.

There are also saddle fitting systems where fitting a saddle wider than normal and using pads in a specific way can help in cases of muscle atrophy. This is a specialist area that calls for a knowledgeable fitter, not a DIY job.

The one thing a numnah can't do is turn a badly fitting saddle into one that fits well, even on a temporary basis. It's also essential to ensure that it doesn't pull down over the withers or at the back, thus applying pressure, but stays up in the gullet. If a numnah has fixing straps, make sure they are in the appropriate place and, if not, ask your saddler to move them so they don't pull it down. One of the best designs for stability – in terms of both staying off the back and helping to keep a well-fitting saddle in place – is the Barnsby Grip numnah, shown in photo 4.11.

Whilst stirrups can't have a direct effect on your horse's comfort and way of going, they can certainly help indirectly by improving your comfort and helping you maintain a correct position. It's sensible to use a safety design

4.10 *left* A numnah should not pull down over the withers or at the back.

4.11 *below* The Barnsby Grip numnah aids saddle stability and stays off the horse's back.

that minimises the risk of your foot being trapped if you fall, but the classic Peacock safety stirrup with a rubber ring on the outside is only suitable for very small children. If used by a larger child or adult, the extra weight puts too much stress on the metal and eventually, it will literally break. The one shown in photo 4.12 as a dire warning was used by a 57 kg (9 stone) teenager for showjumping: fortunately, it broke whilst she was riding on the flat and she managed to keep her seat.

There is now a wide range of designs suitable for adults and in some cases, children. Two of the most popular are the bent leg safety iron (photo 4.13) and the Mountain Horse SCS3 system (photo 4.14). The latter has a release mechanism which opens in an accident and backward-angled, grooved treads. The grooves match those on the soles of boots in the range, to give security and encourage a heels-down position without holding the foot in a locked position.

Other options include stirrups which always rest at an angle that makes them easily retrievable, and those which have hinged emergency release sides. Hinged and multi-jointed irons are often kinder to the rider's joints, more comfortable when jumping and riding for long periods and also minimise the chance of a foot being trapped in a fall.

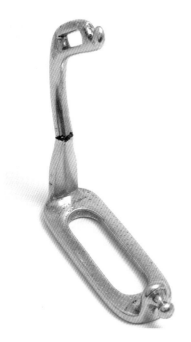

4.12 This Peacock safety iron broke under the stress of a 57 kg (9 stone) rider's weight – proof that it should only be used for small children.

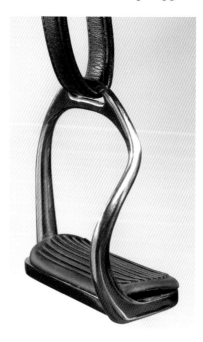

4.13 The bent leg safety iron is a popular design and suitable for adults and younger riders.

4.14 The Mountain Horse SCS3 system combines safety and stability for the rider.

Common sense tells us that a girth which is fastened too tightly or which has the buckles at the wrong height will cause discomfort. We also know, thanks to research by Australian scientists, that too tight a girth restricts the horse's stride length – which has all sorts of knock-on effects, from altering his overall posture to limiting a racehorse's speed. This means that designs which incorporate stretch and so 'breathe' with the horse are preferable, though you need to make sure that the stretch is distributed evenly and not via elastic inserts at one end only.

Short dressage girths designed to minimise the bulk under the rider's legs must still be long enough to ensure that, when adjusted to the optimum length, the buckles rest above the horse's elbows. Some riders use girths that are too short, so that the buckles catch the horse at every stride. Short and standard-length girths which are shaped to avoid pinching the elbow are useful, but you still need to remember to stretch your horse's forelegs forward before you mount, to prevent folds of skin getting pinched.

Bits

There are literally thousands of bits on the market, which can be both a good thing and a bad thing. On the positive side, it should be possible to find the right combination of cheekpiece and mouthpiece for any horse, no matter what his mouth conformation, stage of training and way of going. However, the negative side is that it's easy to get totally confused and/or to be persuaded that every new idea is an improvement.

It can also be tempting to assume that somewhere there is a bit that will solve all your problems or persuade your horse to go instantly on the bit, as if by magic. Sorry: it's a nice idea, but it doesn't work, no matter how clever the marketing or how fervent the endorsement from a top rider.

However, there is no doubt that making sure your horse's mouth and teeth are in good condition and thinking about whether the bit you use is appropriate for his mouth conformation and stage of training are important and that sometimes, a change can bring about good results. You may also want to look at whether the bit you use suits you as a rider: this may sound strange, but what one rider regards as a good 'feel' doesn't fit in with what another finds appropriate. Obviously what matters most is the horse's comfort and response, but the fact remains that some bits and some riders' hands just don't go together.

For instance, some riders prefer a definite feel and find it difficult to ride any horse in a bit that tends to move more in the horse's mouth, such as a loose-ring bit, and they may tend to set their hands to try to compensate. Others may always feel that a bit which falls into a more static category, such as an eggbutt snaffle, has a 'dead' feel and be tempted to ride with busy hands. As mentioned earlier, novice or uneducated riders may use their hands without even being aware of it and in this case, a bit which remains as stable as possible in the horse's mouth – and help from an instructor to improve their technique – will usually cause less discomfort.

Mouth conformation

The shape of your horse's mouth, both inside and out, affects the type of bit he will be comfortable with. Although it's often said that a thick bit is milder than a thinner one, because it has a greater bearing surface, this isn't necessarily true. If a horse doesn't have room for a thick mouthpiece, he won't be able to close his mouth properly and as well as being uncomfortable he will have a dry mouth. This, in turn, means that the bit won't slide over the bars of the mouth, but will be more likely to rub against the skin covering them.

The conformation of his mouth and lips affects the design of the mouthpiece he will be comfortable with in other ways, too. From the outside, see whether his lips are fleshy and wrinkle easily or not, and whether he is short from the end of his muzzle to the corners of his lips.

Look at the corners of his lips, inside and out, for signs of rubs or pinching. When you gently part his lips, does he have a thick tongue that bulges out between his teeth on each side? If so, this will restrict the amount of room for a bit and, again, will often make a thick mouthpiece inappropriate.

Horses, like people, have individual points of mouth conformation and different breeds and types often have common denominators. For instance, cobs often have short mouths coupled with thick necks and although it is possible to find snaffles with which they are comfortable, they often go nicely in pelhams (although the latter can't be used in dressage competitions). To get the best communication with a pelham, it should be used with two reins so that you can apply minimum leverage with the top rein and ask for more flexion with a gentle signal on the bottom one, which applies a little more poll pressure and also briefly activates the curb chain.

Some horses have relatively low palates; this is something often found in Arabs and Connemaras, though they are not alone. If you rest your finger gently on the bars of a horse's mouth and crook it slightly, you will be able to judge how much room he has, though obviously you need to be able to compare different horses. A horse with a low palate will often be far more comfortable in a double or multi-jointed bit than a single-jointed one.

The best person to tell you about the conformation and condition of your horse's mouth is a qualified equine dental technician or a vet who has made a special study of dentistry. Unfortunately, the latter are few and far between and, in the UK, a British Equine Veterinary Association accredited EDT will often have more experience. Although you can spot signs of problems near the corners of the lips, the only way to see exactly what's going on is with the use of a dental gag – otherwise, you run the risk of getting bitten.

Fit for the job

Are you sure that your bit is the correct size and adjusted at the correct height? That might sound like an obvious question, but at any event where there is a large group of horses and riders there are plenty of examples of bits that don't fulfil one or sometimes both of these requirements. The commonest mistake is to use a bit with a jointed mouthpiece that is too long. This means that even when it is adjusted at the correct height, the joint will lie too low in the mouth and, because it can move too far from side to side, it will often not lie centrally. Both problems affect the horse's comfort and mean you aren't giving the correct signals.

Whatever the design of a mouthpiece, it should be long enough to prevent the cheekpieces or rings rubbing or pinching the corners of the mouth, but not so long that it slides excessively from side to side. A bit with fixed cheeks – of which the most common examples are the eggbutt, fixed cheek and D-ring – should fit snugly without pinching. As a guideline, when it is pulled gently to one side so that one cheek is flat against the corners of the mouth and any joints are straightened, there should be a gap between the cheekpiece and the other side of no more than 1 cm (0.4 inch). With a loose-ring bit, you may need to allow slightly more, depending on how fleshy the horse's lips are, to avoid pinching.

When a bit is the correct height in the horse's mouth, it should lie comfortably across the bars. You don't want to see the corners of the lips pulled upwards into a false smile, but nor should the bit be low enough to allow or encourage the horse to put his tongue over it. The risk of the latter is greater with a single-jointed bit than with a mullen mouth, double-jointed or multi-jointed one. If a horse has particularly fleshy lips, you may get a wrinkle at the side of the mouth when the bit is at the correct height.

Sometimes, a tiny adjustment of one hole on just one side will make a big difference to the way your horse accepts the bit. If you make an alteration this way, gently straighten the bridle so that the bit lies level.

New ideas

Over the first decade of this century, there have been many new ideas in bitting. Some have proved themselves beyond doubt, whilst others have perhaps been more successful in theory than in practice. There have also been fashions that have come and gone, often within a particular sport such as showjumping or showing. No one can claim to have the definitive answer or to have identified the best design, but there are some designs and applications you might want to consider.

Many horses go better in double-jointed mouthpieces than ones with single joints. The French link snaffle, with a kidney-shaped central link, is a classical design that suits many horses, but lozenges are said to be gentler on the tongue. Bits with angled lozenges, marketed under names such as the Ultra KK, may apply a more definite signal but without the pressure of a Dr Bristol, which has a flat plate and is not permitted under FEI dressage rules. Check whether a bit needs to be positioned in a certain way: the Ultra KK (which is dressage-legal) has an arrow which must be on the left-hand side, facing forwards.

Some trainers are now taking a new look at the Waterford snaffle, which has a multi-jointed mouthpiece (see photo 4.17). At one time, it was generally classed as a severe bit because riders found it often made it easier for

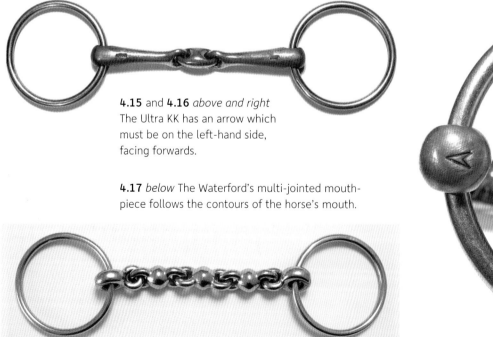

4.15 and **4.16** *above and right* The Ultra KK has an arrow which must be on the left-hand side, facing forwards.

4.17 *below* The Waterford's multi-jointed mouthpiece follows the contours of the horse's mouth.

them to control strong horses. You could discuss forever whether or not horses are strong or riders make them that way, but the fact is that a Waterford follows the shape of the horse's mouth and may, therefore, simply be more comfortable for him

The material a bit's mouthpiece is made from can also encourage a horse to accept it more happily. As has already been explained, a reasonably wet mouth means the bit will be lubricated and some plastic compounds, sweet iron and metals with a copper content encourage salivation.

If your horse suddenly starts resisting a bit he has been working in quite happily, and you haven't increased your demands on him, check the state of the bit as well as the state of his mouth and teeth. Some materials are inevitably damaged by horses' teeth and over time, all bits are liable to wear. A cheap bit may be a bargain, or it may be badly made from poor-quality materials – joints can pinch and the holes of loose-ring snaffles may have rough edges.

Myler bits

Whilst it's appropriate in the context of this book to discuss bits in fairly general terms, you can't get away from the Myler phenomenon. At first dismissed by many English-style riders as 'cowboy bits,' they have won many converts and certainly made a lot of people think about how bits work. Whether or not one of the designs in the range will always be the best choice is open to debate – and perhaps depends as much on whether a rider can use them according to the designers' principles as on their construction – but there is a logic to their design.

Great emphasis is put on making sure that pressure is dispersed correctly and that the horse has enough tongue room to be able to swallow. All the mouthpieces are curved, and joints are covered by barrel-shaped sleeves to prevent pinching or a nutcracker action. Cheeks are available with slots (which the inventors call hooks). The top slot takes pressure off the tongue and stabilises the bit and it is said that when the rein slot is used, it allows sufficient but minimal tongue pressure.

The final design point in most Myler bits is that one side of the bit moves without the other, using the barrel as a pivot. Arguably, this happens in traditional jointed designs, but perhaps not so efficiently and without giving such a clear signal – and, just as important, without pushing the centre joint down on the tongue.

The Myler combination bit is one of the most controversial in the range, but only because many people do not appreciate how it works and assume it is severe. In fact, the reverse is true and it gives control because it has a kind action. Control points are dispersed around the nose and mouth and many horses who are strong in conventional bits seem to go kindly in it. Some trainers also like to use it at an early stage in a horse's education and then to move on to a bit without the supplementary control points; logically, this would be one in the Myler range, such as a comfort snaffle.

4.18 This Myler Comfort snaffle has hooks (slots) to take bridle cheekpieces and reins. At present it is not dressage-legal, but the version without the hooks is.

4.19 and **4.20** *below left and right* The Myler combination bit disperses control points around the mouth and nose and has a kind rather than a severe action.

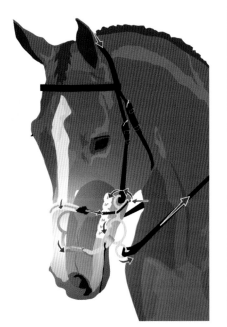

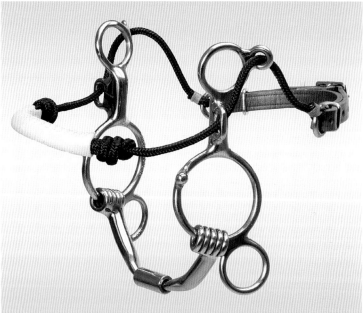

The combination noseband is made from rawhide and soft rope, with knots at each side that are said to help with steering. The bit, which again allows room for the horse's tongue, can have either a long or short shank.

If you want nose pressure to take precedence over action from the bit, adjust the noseband more tightly; if you want the bit to act first and to gradually introduce nose pressure, start with the noseband on its loosest setting and tighten it gradually.

Going bitless

At one time, bitless bridles were generally viewed as something you had to use when nothing else seemed to work, or a horse had temporary discomfort in his mouth because of teething or minor injury. Now, some riders prefer them because they feel they are kinder than using a bit; that isn't true of all designs, some of which can exert considerable leverage, but it's a subject that causes much controversy.

Whatever your views, you may want to use one when introducing a young horse to being ridden, or to check your riding technique. Riding without a bit enables you to accustom the horse to carrying weight and to start learning how to adjust his balance accordingly, without the risk of putting too much pressure on his mouth. It's also a salutary experience to do this with a horse who is normally ridden in a bit, as it can highlight the traps we all tend to fall into by letting rein signals dominate – in particular, using too much inside rein to ask for turns and on circles and thus forcing the horse to go crooked.

Designs of bitless bridles vary in their action and with a young horse, it's best to use one which does not employ potentially powerful leverage. In particular, this rules out the German hackamore, though there are horses, riders and circumstances for which this is suitable. When starting out, try either a Dually halter, a Blair or English pattern bitless bridle, a Parelli hackamore or a Dr Cooke bitless bridle.

4.21 *below left* A hackamore with the rein loose and **4.22** *below centre* with the rein activated (see arrows). The Blair or English pattern bitless bridle is one of the simplest designs.

4.23 *below* The Parelli hackamore is used as part of the Parelli system and bears a strong resemblance to very early designs.

Bridles

To try to keep things as clear as possible, bits have been dealt with as a subject on their own – but at the same time, you need to think about the bridle you use. In particular, is it the right size and correctly adjusted and, if you use a noseband to help influence your horse's way of going or give extra control, are you using the right one?

It isn't rocket science to work out that a bridle which pinches the horse's ears or rubs against his facial bones is going to make him uncomfortable, but you'll see many examples of both scenarios. The commonest mistakes are browbands which are too short and pull the headpiece forward on to the base of the ears; nosebands which are too flimsy or where the section which goes across the front of the nose is too short; throatlatches which are too tight. If a horse is really unlucky, you might see all these errors!

The basic guidelines for a well-fitting bridle are:

- The browband should be long enough to prevent the ears being pinched, but not so long that it flops up and down.

- There should be at least a finger's width between the top of a cavesson noseband, or the cavesson part of a Flash, and the bottom of the facial bones. It should not be so tight that it prevents the horse from opening his mouth enough to mouth the bit, a point which also applies to other designs (see below).

4.24 A well-fitting snaffle bridle with correctly adjusted Flash noseband.

- You should be able to fit the width of four fingers between the throatlatch and the horse's cheek to allow him to flex without restriction.

Over the past few years, there has been increasing interest in bridles designed to remove pressure points at the poll and nose, such as the Elevator bridle and the Albion KB. Another new idea is the Rambo Micklem Multibridle, already mentioned in Chapter 2, which puts no pressure on the facial bones, poll or cheek tissues.

4.25 *above* You should be able to fit four fingers between the throatlatch and the horse's cheek.

4.26 *right* The Albion KB bridle avoids concentrated pressure on the poll and nose.

Open or closed?

Whilst no one wants to see a horse opening his mouth wide to evade the bit (or, more accurately, the rider's hands) he needs to be able to mouth the bit and relax his jaw to be comfortable and to work correctly. Unfortunately, some riders become so fixated on keeping their horses' mouths closed that they strap them shut.

So, if you feel you need to use a Flash, Grakle or drop noseband, don't fasten it so tightly the horse suffers from tack-induced lockjaw. With a Flash, make sure the cavesson part is substantial enough not to slip down the horse's face in use and with a drop, check that the top strap is on, not below, the facial bones. If it rests on the fleshy part underneath, it will restrict the horse's breathing – and no matter how you may feel sometimes, this is not a good idea!

If a horse repeatedly opens his mouth, there could be one or a combination of reasons. He could be demonstrating that he's uncomfortable, that you're using too strong hands, that he finds what you're asking him to do is difficult or that he wants to go faster than you do. If it's a schooling 'problem', you can often achieve a lot by going back a stage and looking at the way you are riding.

At the same time, you need to feel safe and in control, without giving the horse more to fight against. A high-ring Grakle, which doesn't press on the cheek teeth, or a noseband which fastens above and below the bit but which incorporates elasticated inserts, may be more successful than other designs.

Training aids

Just as there are no magic bits, so there are no magic gadgets that will turn a horse who is heavy on the forehand and/or pokes his nose into one who goes in self-carriage. However, that isn't a reason to condemn all training aids – which is what all such equipment *should* be.

In any case, where do you draw the line between standard equipment and training aids? In the broadest sense, martingales, neckstraps and side reins are all training aids, yet they are far more socially acceptable than many other ideas. In a perfect world, every rider should be able to train every horse to go correctly using nothing more than the most basic equipment. In the real one, there are horses, riders and situations where extra help is needed to show a horse how you are asking him to work. This applies particularly to a horse who has developed evasions or resistances because of incorrect riding or lack of correct training.

There isn't room to detail all the training aids available and their use, though some have been referred to in Chapter 2. Personally, I wouldn't use anything that didn't reward the horse by stopping its action immediately he obeyed it – and didn't rely on the rider or person lungeing to do this. For this reason, I would never use draw or running reins.

Use the following points as food for thought when choosing and using equipment.

- Your horse must be sound and his mouth, teeth, back and feet must be in good condition. The exception is when a horse has been diagnosed by a vet as having a particular problem and you have been advised to use a particular training aid, such as a Chambon, as part of a rehabilitation problem.

- Check whether equipment is recommended for lungeing, riding or both. An increasing number of people are riding horses with side reins fitted, perhaps because they assume that because they are usually fitted for lunge lessons, this is safe practice. It isn't – a horse used for lunge lessons is by definition obedient to lunge and is under the control of the trainer, not the rider. If you ride a horse with side reins without him being lunged – and therefore controlled from the ground – there is a risk that if he bucks or spooks, he may lose his balance or resist to the extent that he, his rider, or both suffer a fall. As he won't be able to use his head and neck to balance properly, the consequences can be severe and even fatal; there have been instances of horses breaking their necks this way. There have also been accidents where riders have become caught up in side reins and dragged.

- As all horses can be alarmed by the feel of something new, introduce equipment carefully and fit it fairly loosely to start with. For instance, even experienced horses can be startled when they first experience the feel of training aids which pass behind and round their quarters.

- Training aids which attach to the bit should only be used with some form of simple snaffle, not one which employs poll pressure or leverage.

- Only work the horse for short periods to start with, because you are asking him to use different muscles and he will find it tiring. If you overdo an exercise session, or ache a little because you have done something different, you can ease off the next day. If your horse feels the same way and you ask him to work as hard or harder, the only way he can tell you how he feels is by resisting. A training aid should be productive, not counterproductive.

- Along the same lines, unless you are carrying out a specific veterinary-supervised programme, alternate work days with days when you hack out, turn the horse out to graze, or both.

- A training aid won't make your horse work on the bit, but if used as part of a correct training programme, it will help him build up the muscles to enable him to do so. A lot of equipment influences a horse's head-carriage, but to be on the bit and in self-carriage he needs to work from behind and lift his abdominal muscles: see the suggested lungeing programme in Chapter 2.

Simple and successful aids

Some of the most useful training aids are so simple they tend to get over-looked. In some cases, they are designed for riders as much as for horses, which is an excellent reason for using them.

A neckstrap, which can be either a spare stirrup leather buckled round the horse's neck or the neckstrap of a martingale or breastplate, is more than a grab handle. It can be used to help introduce or emphasise downward transitions and half-halts without putting pressure on the horse's mouth and also to make sure you aren't relying too much on your reins to steer.

As you ask your horse to slow down from your body position, *without pulling back on the reins*, slip your fingers under the neckstrap and give a short pull on it. To test whether you're cheating on steering, hold the neck-strap as well as the reins; use your weight and leg aids and keep your hands as a pair as you turn.

The Mailer Bridging Rein (photo 4.27) is also a useful multi-purpose training aid. Designed by showjumping trainer Carol Mailer primarily to help riders who lose stability and allow their reins to become gradually longer when jumping, it is also useful for reminding you to use your hands as a pair when schooling on the flat. Based on the bridging rein technique used by jockeys, it comprises a pair of reins with grips that take a bridging loop to link left to right.

Fasten the bridging loop slightly further back from where you normally hold the reins when they are adjusted correctly. You can then hold them as normal, but if the horse or pony pulls forward or down, you have a bridging position without bulk that gives you stability and therefore control without pulling back.

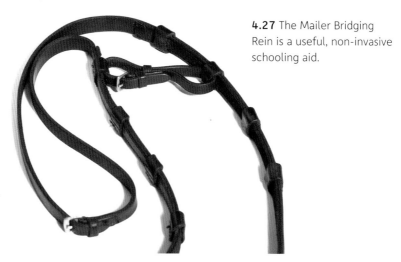

4.27 The Mailer Bridging Rein is a useful, non-invasive schooling aid.

Problem-solving strategies with tack

Improving your horse's way of going or solving problems is obviously not just a case of changing your tack. However, there are guidelines that can help your overall strategy, as shown by the following examples set around the basic problems which underlie most communication breakdowns.

Problem: Horse feels heavy in the hand or is 'dead' in the mouth

Suggestions

- If you have been using a bit with fixed cheeks, which stays relatively still in the mouth, try one with loose rings. In cases where steering still leaves something to be desired, use rubber bitguards (biscuits) to keep the bit central.

- Make sure the horse understands how to respond to the bit by working him from the ground (see Making the Mouth in Chapter 7) and include lots of transitions in your schooling and hacking out.

- Make sure he is going forward and introduce or include exercises suitable for his level of training to increase the activity of his inside hind leg, such as those suggested in Chapter 7. Whilst we all want to ride with the classical 'elastic contact', make sure you are not fiddling with the reins to try and get the horse 'off the hand': instead, think of getting him 'off the leg'.

4.28 Rubber bitguards help keep a bit central.

Problem: Horse is unwilling to work forward into a contact

Suggestions

- Try a bit that is more stable in the mouth. This could be one with an unjointed mouthpiece in plastic or metal or, if your horse responds better to one with a joint or joints, a bit with fixed cheeks. A correctly fitted running martingale may assist by helping to keep the bit stable.

- Lungeing with side reins helps give some horses confidence, though others find it easy to 'come behind them' and so continue to avoid working forward to a contact. In this case, a Lungie Bungie (see Chapter 2) may be more appropriate. This allows more lateral flexion and may offer more encouragement.

- Check that you are not trying to 'take' a contact by getting hold of the front end instead of setting an appropriate rein length, keeping still hands and encouraging the horse to work forwards.

Problem: Horse is strong

Strategies

A lot of riders describe their horses as 'strong', but one person's definition is not always the same as another's. Before you start thinking about possible strategies, define your problem more clearly by asking yourself a few questions.

- Is your horse always against your hand, pulling and/or yanking on the reins, or does he become excited in certain circumstances, such as when he is ridden with other horses?

- Does he become strong because he always wants to go faster than you do?

- Is he unbalanced and heavy in your hand? In this case, he isn't really 'strong', but is leaning on your hands to try to hold himself up.

- Is he unbalanced and also wanting to go faster, either because he is keen or, alternatively, because he is nervous? Some horses worry when they lose their balance and rush to try to regain it. Again, these animals should not be described as 'strong'.

- Is he a balanced but powerful and onward-bound horse who is, perhaps, either beyond your present level of ability or simply the sort of ride you don't enjoy or feel comfortable on?

- Are you helping him or hindering him? If you have a secure seat and good balance, you will be able to control him more through your posture than through the reins.

Suggestions

The first thing you need to look at is your horse's overall schooling and the way you ride him, ideally with help from a good trainer who can suggest ways of improving your horse's balance and responsiveness and, if necessary, improve your confidence. If you feel a horse wants to go faster than you do – even if that isn't strictly the case and it's down to lack of balance – the natural reaction is to take a tighter hold on the reins. Unfortunately, this is counterproductive and what you need to do is improve your horse's balance, responsiveness and calmness.

When you've identified the cause of your problems, you can work on ways to solve them. This will include looking at diet and management, as discussed in Chapter 3. From the point of view of tack, you need to find a compromise where you feel you are in control, but where your horse is comfortable and not unduly restricted. There is a lot of truth in the old saying that 'It takes two to pull', but it's also true that you need to be able to feel confident that you don't have to get into this situation.

The simple but effective Mailer Bridging Rein is a good starting point, especially if you are using a dressage-legal snaffle and don't want to change. It often breaks the cycle of the horse pulling the rider off balance, then the rider pulling back at the horse, and so on.

Don't feel guilty if you do think you need to use a different bit. In some cases, this may be a full-time change and in others, it may be just for particular scenarios such as hacking in company, or jumping. You don't have to think in terms of using a more severe bit, because a bit is only as mild or severe as the person holding the reins. For instance, a mullen mouth pelham with two reins is a better option in light hands than a snaffle in heavier ones. Many horses respond to it well and are less inclined to lean and, as a result, their riders don't set themselves against them.

You don't get the same subtlety by using a pelham with a single rein and couplings, since two reins allow you to alter the signals, but it's a set-up that works for some horses or ponies, and some riders.

If you use a snaffle and want to keep the continuity, a different mouthpiece may help. The Myler system offers many options, though you need to talk to someone trained to understand the range and, ideally, who can see you and your horse working. Some riders find that using a Dr Bristol helps with horses who become strong cross-country; this has a flat-sided central link but, unlike the French link snaffle, is not dressage-legal.

Other designs which might be worth considering are snaffles with rollers set round the mouthpiece. These not only discourage a horse from leaning, but encourage him to relax his jaw by giving him something to play with. A Waterford snaffle is also accepted readily by some horses.

Different noseband designs may help dissuade a horse from opening his mouth too wide but, as always, it's important not to try to fasten his jaws shut. Similarly, a correctly fitted running martingale may help by keeping the bit on the bars of the mouth and acting as a buffer between the bit and the rider's hands if the horse throws up his head.

Chapter **Five**

Manners

S YOUR HORSE POLITE AND pleasant to live with? If not, it's time to do something about it. You wouldn't put up with ill-mannered behaviour from family or friends, so there's no reason why you should put up with it from your horse.

Equine/human relationships

A lot of people allow their horses to push them around and literally walk all over them and seem to accept that this is normal behaviour. It isn't: you will want to have a partnership with your horse, but someone has to call the shots. That someone has to be you.

Horses are herd animals and in any herd, there is a hierarchy. Everyone knows his or her place and when they remain within them, everyone is happy. There will, of course, be challenges and sometimes positions in the ranks change, but there is always one horse who is boss. This means that your horse has to look to you as his herd leader, though it is a relationship that should still allow for mutual respect.

Being a leader means that you set the ground rules and you make decisions. However, you also have to make sure that you explain to your horse what the rules are and that he understands them, and that you are consistent in asking him to stay within the boundaries that are imposed.

If you're dealing with a very young horse, it's important to remember that behaviour that might seem funny or cute when he is a foal or yearling may not be so appealing when he's a strapping three- or four-year-old. I know one normally sensible and generally knowledgeable owner who thought it was delightful to kneel down, pick up her Shetland foal's forefeet and place them on her shoulders; two years later, when he thought it was great fun to rear up and try and do the same thing, she wished she'd listened to everyone who had told her it wasn't a good idea.

Ideally, all horses and ponies are taught good manners from the start. In practice, this doesn't always happen. Some are backed and ridden with scant attention paid to everyday handling and others are handled inconsistently or incorrectly, so what should seem like simple tasks become difficult.

Horses don't automatically tie up quietly and they don't automatically pick up their feet. In fact, when they learn to do these things, they are performing tasks that are against their instincts, as a horse is vulnerable when he is restricted. When he has one foot off the ground, he is particularly vulnerable, as not only is he restricted, but he has to learn to adjust his balance. Also, in the wild, falling over is potentially very dangerous for a horse – so if he feels under threat of this happening as a result of being off balance, he will feel very insecure. If a handler doesn't give him time to stand comfortably before he is asked to lift a foot, or lifts a leg too high from the ground, he can't be expected to acquiesce calmly.

Good manners don't just make horses nicer to live with, they keep you safe. Who wants to get flattened by a horse who barges out the stable door as soon as it is opened, or risk twisting an ankle because a horse tows you out to the field? Why risk getting your toes trodden on by a horse who doesn't respect your space?

A well-mannered horse should be obedient and calm when asked to do the following:

- Be touched all over by a handler who gives him warning and touches him confidently and quietly, without poking or dabbing at him.

- Pick up his feet in turn when asked, without resisting or kicking.

- Stand still when tied up.

- Lead on a loose rein or rope quietly, keeping the appropriate distance from the handler and obeying immediately when asked to turn, stop or back up.

- Move back from the stable door when it is opened, not trying to crowd you as you go in, or push his way out.

- Move sideways in either direction when asked.

Your part of the bargain is that you should:

- Always remain calm and give your horse time to obey an instruction.

- Be consistent, even when you're in a hurry.

- Handle him quietly but firmly, without taking him by surprise. For instance, don't walk up to a horse, get hold of his fetlock and expect him to pick up his foot. If he does, it means he has better manners than you!

Remember, too, that horses have a 'blind spot' directly in front of their nose, so try to approach your horse from the side. It's also a good idea to speak gently to him before you touch him, especially if you think his attention may be elsewhere.

As soon as he does as you ask, reward him. A reward can be as simple as releasing the pressure on the lead rope, or it may be a scratch at the withers or a soft word. Although some experts in clicker training like to use food as a reward, it isn't recommended that you do so unless you are working under expert supervision, as your horse may start to focus on the food rather than you and may be more inclined to push or nip.

Another thing to think about is whether you are causing problems by paying your horse unwanted attention. Whilst it's always nice to have a horse who responds to attention, some don't like being fussed over and find it irritating. If your horse gives you this message, respect it. You may find that once you respect his signals, he will eventually turn to you if he wants attention – and when that happens, it is really rewarding.

Equipment for ground training

Handling or 'ground training' work is done whilst the horse is wearing a headcollar or halter. In some cases, a plain headcollar is fine; in others, you may get better results by using a specialist design. These are often referred to under the generic term of pressure halter, but there are differences that should be appreciated when choosing which one to use.

All headcollars and halters apply pressure, but some act more strongly on different points than others. A well-fitting leather or nylon headcollar acts on the nose, so this is the control point most horses become accustomed to from their early days. A halter made from fairly thin, knotted yachting rope – often called a horseman's halter – will act on the nose, the sides of the face (where the knots may act as a steering aid) and in some cases, the poll. In some designs, metal plates at the poll put extra pressure on that sensitive area; opinions on them vary, but I would worry about the risk of causing pain or damage.

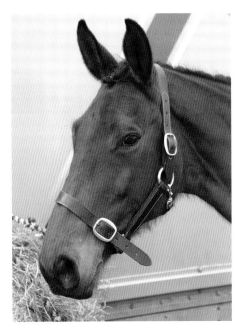

5.1 *left* A well-fitting leather headcollar – this one was made to measure for this event horse.

5.2 *right* The knots on this rope halter help with steering.

Other rope halters are designed to tighten round the nose and over the poll when either the handler, or the horse's negative actions, apply pressure. When the horse obeys the handler's instructions, or stops pulling, running backwards or whatever has caused the pressure, the halter should immediately loosen and so the pressure stops immediately. In skilled hands and safe surroundings, these halters may be useful, but if the design or the handler is slow to release the pressure, they can cause as many problems as they solve.

Everyone has a favourite and my preference when needing clearer, more definite signals than an ordinary headcollar can give is for a Dually headcollar, designed by American trainer Monty Roberts, or a horseman's halter – usually in that order. The Dually headcollar (photo 5.3) has two applications: when you fasten the rope to the back ring, it acts in a very similar way to a standard headcollar, though because the rear strap is lower than the front one, it is slightly more effective. However, when you attach the rope to one of the rings on the sliding ropes across the front of the nose, you get a smooth, free-running 'pressure and release' action.

Never tie up a horse using anything other than a standard headcollar. If he pulls back, he will meet instant pressure and if he panics and carries on pulling, he could hurt or frighten himself. It isn't worth the risk, even if – as is always advised –

5.3 *below* Attaching the rope to one of the rings on the sliding ropes across the front of the nose on a Dually headcollar gives a free-running 'pressure and release' action.

you tie the lead rope to a string loop or use one of the breakaway devices on the market. You can tie up a horse in a Dually headcollar as long as you use the back ring, but you need to keep the horse in view. Although it carries a warning label telling you not to use the training rings for this purpose, there could still be a slight risk that one could get caught up on something if you leave a horse unsupervised, even when the tying-up rope goes to the back ring.

For most in-hand work, it's best to use a rope rather than a long lunge line, simply because you don't have to cope with a handful of coiled line. However, if you feel safer using a lunge line and can manage it, by all means do so. A happy medium is to use a rope or line that is about 3.7 m (12 ft) long. Whatever you choose, make sure it's easy to handle – nylon webbing is cheap, but it's usually too lightweight and can be uncomfortable to handle even when wearing gloves. (Whatever you're doing, and however well you know your horse, wear gloves and sensible footwear. It's also a good idea to wear a hat.)

Making the right moves

Teaching your horse to lead politely, to stop, start and steer when and how you want him to and to move away from you when you ask him will make life much easier and pleasanter for both of you. You need to make sure that *he* is the one doing the moving, even if it sometimes seems simpler to let him stand still whilst you move out the way – because if you let him dictate who makes the effort, you are letting him take the dominant role. Opinions vary on how intelligent or otherwise horses are, but they learn from repetition, whether the lesson is good or bad!

In the context of training, 'dominant' does not mean aggressive; it means you are taking the role of leader. A good first lesson to work on is to get your horse to back up in hand, which reinforces this. You can do this in a large stable and/or in a safe working environment, such as an arena or fenced-off schooling area.

In the stable, fit your headcollar or halter and rope and stand in front of and slightly to one side of your horse. Some trainers will stand directly in front, but this means that your horse may not see you properly and if he does step forward or barge, you are in a vulnerable position.

Apply light but clear backward pressure on the rope and if he moves back, just a step, make sure it is released completely. If he doesn't move, increase the pressure and press your fingers into his chest without jabbing at him. Again, as soon as he takes a step back, release all pressure and reward him. Repeat until the horse steps back readily at light pressure on the rope.

Your accompanying body posture will increase your powers of persuasion. Instinctive trainers have always used body posture to influence horses, often without realising it, but in recent years high-profile trainers have explained how and why it works. There are many excellent books and DVDs that go into great depth, but the basics are simple and logical.

If you square your shoulders, look at your horse and make yourself physically 'big', he is more likely to stop or move back: if you lower your shoulders, turn sideways on and don't look straight at him, you will encourage a hesitant horse to come towards you or be easier to catch. This means that squaring your shoulders and looking at your horse as you step towards him and apply pressure on the rope makes the message clearer.

The next stage is to ask him to step towards you, again by applying pressure on the rope and releasing it as soon as he responds. It's important that he doesn't feel blocked, so it's often better to do this outside. Again, don't stand directly in front of him – not only for safety reasons, but because you are physically blocking his movement. Have you ever seen someone having difficulty persuading a horse to load, standing on the ramp in front of the horse, pulling on a rope and wondering why he won't go forward?

This time, step back and, without squaring your shoulders or looking directly at the horse, apply pressure on the rope to ask him to come towards you. As soon as he steps forward, release the pressure and reward.

You should also make sure that your horse steps away from you, to either side, when asked. In the stable, or in a safe, enclosed area outdoors, stand at his left shoulder and turn his head slightly towards you, then press and release your fingers against his side just behind the girth. If he makes the slightest shift sideways, reward him. If he doesn't understand, turn his head more towards you whilst you ask with hand pressure, as he is more likely to step sideways to rebalance himself. Repeat from the other side. See photos 5.4a and b overleaf.

This not only makes it easier whilst you are working around your horse; it introduces the idea of moving away from the rider's leg. (Of course, if he already understands the aids for turn on the forehand, he should readily accept being asked to move sideways on the ground.) With a young horse, who hasn't reached that stage in his ridden education, it's a great way of introducing the idea, as it's usually simple to get a helper to give the cue he already understands from the ground whilst you apply the aids.

Some trainers like to use a longer rope – 4.5–6 m (15–20ft) – and flick or whirl the end to get the horse to move his hindquarters sideways. It's up to you whether you use this method, but if you want to use a rope as your main signalling tool, it's best to study the methods and techniques

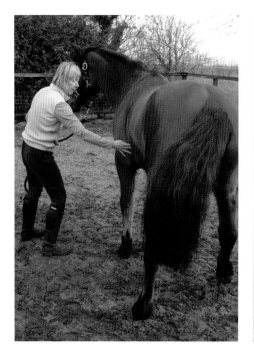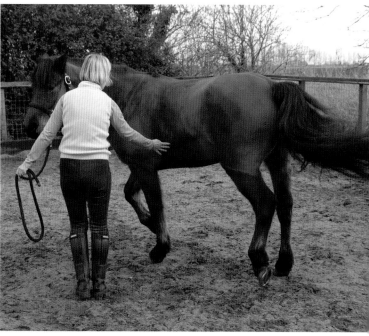

5.4a and **5.4b** Teach the horse to move away from you, to either side, when asked.

of accomplished trainers first rather than start flinging a rope around and either hitting your horse unintentionally, frightening him, or both.

It's also up to you whether or not you use voice commands as well as physical ones. One point of view is that these are superfluous and muddy the water, but horses are so receptive to selective use of the voice that it can be a huge help. The important thing is that it's selective; if someone natters on at you all the time, you tend to tune out, and horses are the same. Most associate simple commands like 'Step back' and 'Over' with the hands-on cues very quickly.

The pressure and release techniques can be used to teach a horse to lead politely in hand. Working in an enclosed area, start alongside the fence and stand at or just in front of the horse's shoulder; although the classical leading position is at the shoulder, many horses get the idea more quickly if you are just in front. Look ahead, think 'Go' and walk off. Ideally, your horse will move off with you and you can ask for halt just before you reach the fence in front of you. Again, ideally your horse will pick up on your body language and stop when you do; more realistically, he'll walk past you and bump against the pressure from the lead rope.

Of course, as horses don't read books, you'll often find that one will lag behind and not want to keep up with you. A nervous horse or one who is unsure of his surroundings may try to tuck in behind your shoulder, but even though this suggests that he accepts you as his 'leader,' it puts you in a vulnerable position – if he spooks, he's likely to jump on top of you, so you need to quietly encourage him to walk alongside. One of the easiest ways to do this is to use light taps with a schooling whip at the same time as giving a verbal command – a click of the tongue is effective -– but it's important to make sure that he isn't frightened of it. Before attempting to use the whip in this way, stroke it gently down his shoulder, then over his body and down his quarters, on both sides, until he is relaxed about the whole thing. If he has been hit with a schooling whip at some time – always a mistake, not only on humane grounds but because it negates a useful signalling tool – this could take time and patience. In some cases, you may have to use a long rope and flick the end against him, instead.

The opposite case is that of the horse who tries to tow you along or, in extreme circumstances, tries to take off, perhaps on the way to the field. Using a control halter or headcollar, walk on and, after just a couple of strides, stop, plant your feet and give a sharp tug on the rope. The resulting bump on the nose should have a salutary effect and you can reward him and repeat; most horses get the message very quickly that it's more comfortable to follow a handler's signals than work to their own agenda.

Tip

If you have an absolute thug who tries to ignore a training headcollar or halter even when it is used correctly – and you're sure he is using his strength to get his own way, rather than reacting through fear – you have to get the message across that this isn't acceptable. One way of doing this is to use a 'hooligan halter' or a chain across the nose.

Whilst it is never acceptable to cause a horse pain, it is better to cause him brief moments of discomfort if the end result is that he learns to listen. Also, if he refuses to listen, you and other people are at risk.

A hooligan headcollar comprises a metal ring attached to a leather head-piece. The ring goes round the nose and has a loop at the back to take the lead rope or rein; if you prefer, you can wrap latex round it. Use it by keeping a slack rein, so there is no pressure on the nose, but if the horse tries his bull-dozer tactics, either plant your feet and let him meet a sharp bump on his nose or, if necessary, give a brief tug and release on the rope.

It's rare to need to use one of these, but I have seen it employed with horses who behaved dangerously and have never known it fail. Giving the horse a bump on the nose seems preferable to pulling him in the mouth, which is likely to be the case in these circumstances if you use a bit.

An alternative, cheaper and less potentially severe option (because it moulds to the nose rather than remaining rigid) is to use a check chain designed for a large dog. Pass it over the front of the nose, through the side rings of the headcollar and fasten your lead rope to both rings at the back of the jaw.

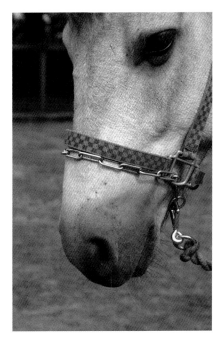 

5.5a and **5.5b** A check chain designed for a large dog can be used with a headcollar to persuade a horse that bulldozer tactics won't work.

Leading safely

It's important to teach a horse to be led from both sides, both to help prevent him becoming one-sided and, more importantly, to ensure that you can lead him on the road safely if necessary. When leading on the road, you should face oncoming traffic and place yourself between the horse and the road – so in the UK and other countries where vehicles are driven on the left, you will be on the left-hand side of the road, leading the horse from his right-hand side.

It is vital to have maximum control in this situation and although you will want to use a headcollar or halter at home, it is generally agreed that when leading a horse on the road, he should wear a bridle and bit. You and he should also be equipped with fluorescent, reflective equipment. Some trainers recommend that horses who do not lead quietly should always be led from a bit and the bottom line is that you must be safe and in control. Although the groundwork explained earlier should help you re-educate a bargy horse, use your common sense.

Some people may advise you to use a Chifney. This is a thin bit which encircles the jaw and is capable of exerting enormous pressure (see photo 5.6). It was designed for the racing industry to give handlers control over stallions and colts with a propensity to rear and whilst there may be situations where it is thought suitable for use in skilled hands, it can't be recommended for general use.

5.6 A Chifney can exert enormous pressure on the jaw and is not recommended for general use.

Perfect pick-ups

It isn't until you come across a horse who refuses to pick up his feet – or even worse, strikes or kicks out at his handler when asked to do so – that you realise how simple and easy life is with an obliging one. However, horses not only have to be taught to pick up their feet; they need to be given the confidence to stand in a vulnerable position. When your instinctive reaction is to run away from danger, standing on three legs is not a good idea.

Horses who have had mud fever are sometimes reluctant to have their legs handled, as they associate this with pain. In bad cases, even touching their legs may cause discomfort or soreness and in others, the necessary task of removing scabs – however gently you try to do it – makes them uncomfortable.

Also, a surprising number of owners are inconsiderate about the way they carry out basic handling, such as picking up feet and grooming. If a horse associates these tasks with an unpleasant experience, such as being off balance or being made uncomfortable in a sensitive area, it's no wonder he is reluctant to comply.

If your horse is reluctant to have his legs handled at all, the only way to solve the problem is to desensitise him. With animals who kick out or strike out, the safe way is to borrow a technique from Monty Roberts – pad out an old glove with straw, fasten it to a long stick and use this to touch the horse's limbs. Stand at a safe distance so that if he lashes out, he can't reach you, but you can keep the 'hand' in contact or replace it immediately afterwards. From there, you can progress to stroking down the leg and eventually replacing the dummy hand with your own.

With horses who are simply reluctant to pick up their feet, you need a mixture of patience and technique. Check that the horse is standing reasonably foursquare, so his weight is distributed evenly, and always warn him what you are going to do by running your hand down the outside of the leg from the shoulder or hindquarters, then slipping it round the fetlock and squeezing gently.

If he doesn't respond, get a helper to gently move him forwards and, keeping your hand in contact with his fetlock, wait until his foot comes off the ground and you can catch hold of his toe. Be content with holding the foot just slightly off the ground to start with and don't pull it forward or back; a lot of people pull their horses' hind legs too far out behind and disturb their balance. After holding his foot for two or three seconds, place it back on the ground.

Remember that if a horse who has previously been happy to pick up his feet suddenly becomes reluctant to do so, it's likely that he is experiencing pain or discomfort in a limb or his back. If the pain is in a limb, it won't necessarily be the one being lifted – it is more likely that he is reluctant to bear more weight on another limb.

Tying up

A horse who refuses to be tied up and pulls back on the rope until he breaks the loop between the rope and the metal tying-up ring is a nuisance and a danger to himself and others. If he gets loose in this way and takes off with a rope flying round his legs, he's likely to trip himself up or be injured, or cause an accident in his panic. Even if he stays calm, he has learned that he can get free this way – and having to put him in a stable every time you want to do something with him is exasperating.

Horses often dislike or are frightened of being tied up simply because they have never been taught to do so. Fortunately, it's usually fairly easy to teach a youngster or to re-educate a breakaway artist, though with the latter, it may always be a risk to leave him tied up unattended, even if you are just nipping to the tack room for something you've forgotten.

Responsible breeders teach horses to tie up when they are just a few months old, but if yours hasn't been educated sufficiently, try a technique used by breeder and international dressage trainer Jennie Loriston-Clarke with foals. She puts her pupil, who has already been taught to wear a head-collar and lead at the side of his dam, in a large stable with plenty of bedding and passes a lunge line through one of the internal wall rings. One end is coiled up in the hand and the other clips to the headcollar and when the foal resists the restriction – as is natural – the handler takes and releases on the rein so he learns that when he stands, the pressure releases. It's a bit like playing a fish on a line, but needs a handler and helper who are calm and capable.

Another technique, used by international event rider Pippa Funnell, is to replace the standard twine loop with a tail bandage, tied to give a stretch loop (see photo 5.7). This has enough give not to frighten the horse but also pro-vides a little resistance and in extreme cases, will break. In most cases, a horse who pulls back reacts much more sensibly when tied to a tail bandage link; if he steps back, you can quietly encourage him forward from the ground. Usually, it takes only a few lessons for him to get the message.

You could also try special breakaway cables, though these are expensive and may be better employed for safety reasons once you've instilled the basic idea of tying up as above. Make sure you use one which stretches before it

5.7 Using a tail bandage as a stretch link can help teach the horse to tie up without pulling back or panicking.

breaks and is covered with a sleeve, so that if it breaks, it does not snap back and hit the horse.

If anyone recommends tying a horse directly to a metal ring or to a telegraph pole, ignore them! I've seen someone tie a horse to a ring in the outer stable wall in the belief that he'd stop pulling when there was no twine loop to break – and find out the hard way that this didn't work. The horse carried on pulling and pulled a plank out of the wall; this snapped back and hit him and he took off in fright, galloping round the yard with a lump of wood banging against him. When he was finally caught, he was trembling with fear, had cuts on his legs – and was even worse to tie up after the experience.

Similarly, it's often said that the best way to 'cure' a horse who is reluctant to tie up is to tie him to a telegraph pole with a stout rope and let him get on with it. Accompanying this advice is the proviso that you should carry a sharp knife so you can cut the rope in an emergency. There are two downsides to this method: one is that even if you use a slip knot, the horse may break his neck before you get chance to free him and the other is that trying to get between a panicking horse and a telegraph pole whilst holding a sharp knife is both dangerous and daft.

Mutual good manners

Teaching your horse good manners isn't about being dominant, it's about establishing a partnership that is pleasant for both of you and increases your confidence in each other. It doesn't take special skills, though you do need patience and the ability to recognise and respond to your horse's reactions.

If in doubt, get expert help – and choose your expert carefully. There are many good trainers and handlers following a variety of approaches, but there may also be self-styled 'gurus' with more marketing skills than practical horse-handling ones.

Always keep safety in mind, especially your own. Although some trainers choose not to wear gloves and/or protective headwear, it's better to be safe than sorry.

Chapter Six

Fitness

BRINGING OUT THE BEST in your horse means allowing and teaching him to work to the best of his ability. To do this, he needs to be fit enough to cope with the job you are asking him to do, whether that is hacking, basic schooling or competing in affiliated competitions. This is common sense, but a lot of riders still take a hit and miss approach to fitness and assume that, for instance, any mature horse can be left in a field all week then cope with three-hour fast hacks or a day of hard competition at the weekend.

There is no such thing as a horse who is fit for every sort of job, because different activities impose different demands. You only have to think in terms of human athletes to realise that just as a 100 metre sprint specialist would not necessarily be able to complete a marathon, so a polo pony would not cope with a long endurance ride, and neither would an endurance horse cope with the demands of polo. However, whatever you are aiming for, a basic fitness programme will give you a firm foundation on which to build.

The time it takes to achieve this basic fitness will vary according to your horse's type, his age and how fit he has been in the recent past. Building up fitness for the first time in a young horse who has just been backed will take longer than getting a horse who has been fit for, say, Pre-novice eventing and then been turned out back to his previous level. Also, horses with a high percentage of Thoroughbred or Arab blood usually reach their desired fitness levels quicker than cobs and other types with a high percentage of cold blood.

It's also important to realise that a horse can be fit without necessarily

6.1 Horses with a high percentage of Thoroughbred or Arab blood – this is a purebred Arab endurance horse – usually reach fitness quicker than those with cold blood.

being supple or athletic; fitness builds strength and stamina, but it takes schooling to build suppleness and balance. A racehorse who is fit enough to run may not be able to canter a 20-metre circle, unless he has an enlightened trainer who realises that the ability to bend and stay in balance can give a horse an advantage in manoeuvrability.

Starting out

Before you start your fitness programme, check that your horse and his equipment are in good shape. If you don't, you may find that a small problem that could have been sorted out quite easily becomes a major one.

Worming and vaccination programmes should be in place and his mouth, teeth and feet should be in good order. If he's fat and woolly and you're starting your fitness programme in mild weather, you may want to clip him to prevent excessive sweating – but take off the minimum amount of hair so that he has the coat over his back and loins to keep him warm. A bib clip, where hair is clipped off the underside of the neck and the chest is usually best (see Chapter 11).

As a horse who is unfit is more prone to rubs, check the condition and fit of your tack: a guide to saddle fitting can be found in Chapter 4. Remember that as he gets fitter, so he will change shape, so check your saddle every couple of weeks and have it adjusted when necessary. I've always found that the Flair air flocking system, whilst quite expensive to install, makes it easier to keep a horse comfortable and avoid pressure points – but, as with traditional wool flocking, it can only be as good as the person adjusting it.

The girth area is particularly prone to pinching, so make sure you tighten the girth gradually and always stretch the horse's legs forward before getting on. Soft, washable girths with stretch throughout their length, or with elastic inserts at each end, are better than ones with no stretch or just one elastic end. If you have to use the latter, put the elastic end on the offside and tighten the girth from the nearside, so you are not tempted to pull it up too tight.

It's also sensible to use protective boots, as an unfit horse is more likely to knock himself. Again, make sure they fit properly and aren't going to rub. Brushing boots are usually adequate; some people like to use knee boots when riding on the road, but the problem with some designs is that, in order to prevent them slipping down, you have to fasten the top straps so tightly they may pinch.

When riding on roads and tracks, always use reflective, fluorescent wear (see Chapter 8). A simple tabard means drivers see you much earlier than if you are wearing drab clothing, and they will hopefully slow down. Research has shown that the most effective combination is a rider wearing a high-visibility waistcoat or tabard and a horse wearing high-visibility boots.

A staged fitness programme

Life would be much easier if we could have a definitive fitness chart and be able to say that a horse will be at a particular stage at a particular week. Because of the variables already mentioned, you can't be regimented in your approach – and, of course, everyday life inevitably gets in the way of cast-iron plans. There's no point in trying to do it totally by the book – this one or any other – and giving yourself a massive guilt complex if work or family commitments get in the way and set your schedule back a few days.

Instead, think in terms of a four-stage plan that will take six to eight weeks. You might find it helps to keep a diary, in which you can make a note of the work you did and how your horse coped. Hopefully, you'll see a continual and gradual improvement, but if you have two or three consecutive days where he seems to find the work hard, it's an indication that you should go back a stage. Getting a horse fit means improving his response to the stresses imposed on his body, but these stresses should be productive, not harmful.

Stage 1

The first stage of any fitness programme is always long, slow distance work (LSD). It isn't a new idea, as in the days when hunters were hunted hard all winter and turned out to grass in the summer, grooms would spend six weeks just walking them. Now, it's accepted that it's better to keep a horse kept solely for hunting 'ticking over' out of season rather than just throwing him out in the field; similarly, most event riders give their horses up to six weeks quiet time at the end of the season, then start work again.

In most cases, spending six weeks in walk is over-cautious, but if your horse is very unfit and you want to be absolutely sure you're doing the right thing, it won't do any harm. There is, of course, one possible problem in restricting your horse to walk: if he's the sort who gets bored or silly after he's had a break, you may have to lunge him for a few minutes before you get on, just to let him get rid of his excess energy. Just a few minutes on each rein, working on a safe surface, should be enough to get his brain in gear. You may, of course, be lucky enough to have access to a horse walker, which makes starting your fitness programme much easier. As with all work, make sure your horse spends the same amount of time on each rein. If you don't have access to a horse walker, start with half an hour in walk under saddle, building up over two or three weeks until you are doing an hour each day.

Although this initial work may seem boring, it's important that you pay attention and keep your horse active. He shouldn't necessarily be on the bit, but nor should he be slopping along, tripping over his own feet and gazing at the scenery.

6.2 A horse walker can be very useful at the start of a fitness programme, but not everyone is lucky enough to have access to one.

Stage 2

Once your horse is coping happily with an hour's active walk, you can start to vary your routine, although – as with any horse at any stage of fitness – you should always spend 10 minutes at the beginning and end of each session in walk to allow him to warm up or cool down. You can now add short schooling sessions to your regime, introducing brief periods of trot and riding easy figures in the school – 20-metre circles, changes of rein, three-loop serpentines and shallow loops. You can also start adding or introducing basic lateral work; in particular, shoulder-in and leg-yielding (see Chapter 7) are useful ways of helping to activate his inside hind leg and increase his overall suppleness.

The trot work should be active, rhythmical and forward – a true working trot that is never rushed or hurried but feels and looks as if it is going somewhere. Whether or not you trot on the road depends on your surroundings; short periods of trot on level roads with a non-slippery surface are generally accepted to be better than trotting on a hard, rutted field or track, but concussion caused by trotting fast or for long periods will do more harm than good. If in doubt, don't.

Advice on getting horses fit usually suggests that one of the best tactics is to ride your horse up hills of gradually increasing steepness. If you can do this, lucky you – working up hills or slopes is a great way of encouraging your horse to push off from his hind legs. Those of us who live in flat areas have to rely on flatwork – in particular, lots of transitions – to achieve this and, once you've worked through Stage 3 and introduced cantering, you can use an interval training programme, as explained later in this chapter.

Lungeing and long-reining can give more variety to your horse's work and you may also want to introduce easy exercises over poles on the ground, as suggested in Chapter 2. This gives both of you something to think about and poles encourage a horse to stretch, look where his going and think about where he is putting his feet.

6.3 *below left* Riding up hills of gradually increasing steepness can be of great benefit when getting a horse fit.

6.4 *below right* Working over poles on the ground encourages a horse to stretch and gives him something different to think about.

Stage 3

If your horse is coping happily with everything you are asking him to do, you can now move on to stage three of your programme – but if you have any doubts, stay at your current level for another week or two, as playing safe at the beginning will bring dividends later on.

All being well, you can now introduce short canter sessions on good going. This can be a mixture of work in the school and out hacking, as long as the ground is not too hard or too boggy or slippery, making canter hacks risky. There's no need to wrap your horse up in cotton wool – in fact, that can be counterproductive, because if he only canters in an arena or on perfect level turf, he'll never cope with normal life. This applies particularly to eventers and endurance horses, who have to work on varied but hopefully decent terrain.

The canter, like the trot, should be balanced and rhythmical. This is less wearing on the horse, as when he canters in rhythm, he breathes in time with his strides. If the canter pattern is disturbed, this has a detrimental impact on his breathing, which won't help the process of improving his fitness. A rhythmical canter also makes it easier for him to do his job: a showjumper or event horse who can't keep the beat is not going to meet his fences on a correct stride and time will be wasted as the rider tries to 'put him right'. If a horse is in a regular rhythm and can lengthen or shorten his stride when asked, this will save time and make things easier for both members of the partnership.

Whilst short periods of canter on the lunge can help if you have a problem getting the correct strike-off (in which case, they should be interspersed with frequent transitions to trot), cantering on the lunge to try to build fitness is not recommended, as it puts a lot of strain on the hocks. Cantering under saddle in the school means you can ensure that the horse is not asked to work on anything smaller than a 20-metre circle, but it's too easy to let circles on the lunge become smaller and smaller in an effort to keep control.

By now, your horse should be ready to go out and take part in a dressage competition at an appropriate level for his stage of training, or a showing class. Even if you are not particularly interested in either, it's a good way of adding variety to his work; you're also increasing the demands on him by travelling him to a show and warming up for a competition.

Stage 4

It's probably now four to six weeks since you started your horse's basic fitness programme and if all has gone according to plan, you'll be ready to start the final stage. This involves asking him to work gradually harder, for longer and sometimes more frequent periods, and enables you to build his cardiovascular fitness by lengthening canter sessions.

You can also borrow from interval training methods. Carry out twice-weekly sessions of 2 minutes in canter followed by 3 minutes in walk, repeated three times. As your horse's recovery rate improves, build this to 3 minutes in canter followed by 3 minutes in walk, again repeated three times.

Keeping the quality of the canter is a priority – it should be energetic and rhythmical, without any exaggerated lengthening of the stride. If you have a stopwatch and can mark out a 400 m (440 yard) distance on reasonable going, practise riding at 350–450 m (380–480 yards) per minute for maximum efficiency.

As your programme progresses, you can vary your horse's regime still further. For instance, three or four schooling sessions a week can be combined with lungeing, hacking, pole work and gymnastic jumping through small grids. Even if you don't want to jump competitively, grid work over low fences is a great way of encouraging your horse to go forward and will also improve his suppleness and reactions. See Chapter 7 for a few simple ideas.

Interval training

If you don't have access to hills, or want a structured fitness programme, you may want to use interval training proper. This centres on set work periods carried out over a specific time, with intervals at walk to allow for a partial recovery. Interval training is not carried out every day, but is a system designed to be incorporated into your overall work regime. The general recommendation is that it is done every four days.

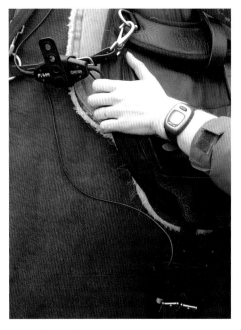

It's a method that has several advantages, as it eliminates guesswork and allows you to make structured increases in your horse's work. Also, because you are working the horse for shorter periods, there is less risk of fatigue and therefore injury. However, the drawback in some cases is that horses can tend to anticipate what comes next and become excited by it – it's the training equivalent of 'This is where we canter' out hacking.

To use interval training, you need one or more 400 m (440 yd) stretches of good going to establish your correct working speed. All-weather gallops are perfect, but only a lucky few have access to these and most riders have to use the edge of a field. You also need either a stopwatch or a watch with a clear second hand, both to time yourself over the distance and to take your horse's pulse and respiratory rates. Event and endurance riders sometimes use heart monitors, which mean they don't have to dismount, but these are expensive.

6.5 Endurance riders often use heart monitors on their horses, which means they don't have to dismount to take the heart rate.

Before starting an interval training programme, you need to have worked through to the end of Stage 3 in the basic fitness programme outlines earlier.

You also need to find your horse's baseline heart rate over a few days; do this by taking his heart rate when he is tacked up and ready for work, and work out an average reading. Don't take a reading before work, when he is at rest, as his heart rate will usually rise slightly when he is ready to work.

Warm him up in walk, then establish the trot you will be working from. Ride your 400 m (440 yard) route at an active but not hurried trot and time how long it takes. You are aiming to cover the distance at a speed of 220 m (240 yards) per minute, which should take 1 minute 49 seconds, so if you are over or under the time, adjust the trot accordingly.

When you've done this, you're ready to start your first session. Warm up in walk, then trot for 2 minutes, walk for 3 minutes to allow a partial recovery, then trot for another 2 minutes before stopping and recording your horse's heart and respiration rates. As soon as you've done this, walk for another 10 minutes, then take the rates again.

Monitoring the rise in your horse's heart rate as he works and the recovery time to the base rate you established earlier allows you to see how your horse is responding to work and recovering from it afterwards. The following guidelines will give you an idea of how he's doing. You're unlikely to need – or be able – to work your horse at the speed of a Thoroughbred racehorse but it's interesting to see the effort required!

6.6 Working at racing speed demands a lot of effort from a horse.

Approximate heart rates (beats per minute)

Resting 35–42

Standing tacked up ready for work 40–65

Active walk 60–80

Active trot 130–50

Canter 120–170

Maximum racing speed 205–240

When your horse has reached the end of his interval training programme – which probably means you are looking at around six weeks to reach Pre-novice event fitness – you can gauge his heart rate after the rest period according to the following:

100 beats per minute – the horse is working reasonably well, but could be asked to work a little harder.

120 beats per minute – a good level to aim for, as it means the horse has worked sufficiently hard and recovered well.

150 beats per minute – this rate is too fast for the horse's stage of fitness. You need to go back a level.

6.7 If your horse has achieved a reasonable fitness level before, it will probably take you around six weeks to build him up to the level when he could cope with a Pre-novice event.

Bring out the BEST IN YOUR HORSE

Take into account the fact that, as interval training works by building up the horse's tolerance to stress, it may be that at first, his heart rate will be higher than 120 bpm – though it shouldn't be as high as 150.

The horse's respiration rate should not be higher than the heart rate. If it is, stop the training session and walk the horse until he recovers. When you are ready to carry out your next session, go back a stage and make sure his recovery rates are normal before increasing the effort.

Over the next few weeks, gradually build up the length of time you trot for and the number of repetitions, until you are carrying out three sessions of trotting for 3 minutes and walking for 3 minutes. Add a final trot session for 3 minutes, then stop and take the heart and respiration rates. Finally, walk for 10 minutes and take them again.

When your horse is recovering well, increase the length of the trot periods to 5 minutes, but reduce the number of repetitions. Trot for 5 minutes and walk for 3; trot for 5 and walk for 3; trot for 5, halt and take his rates; walk for 10 and take the heart and respiration rates again.

Now, provided all is going well, you can introduce canter. First, you need to establish the correct base speed, which is done in the same way you established your trot. This time, you need to ride your 400 m (440 yards) at 350 m (383 yards) per minute, which should take 1 minute, 8 seconds. Whilst you're doing this, you may also want to work out the sort of canter you need to cover the set distance in 1 minute, as you may want to move up to this in your final training sessions.

When bringing in canter work, increase your warm-up period to half an hour in walk and trot. Then canter for 1 minute 8 seconds; trot for 3 minutes; canter for another 1 minute 8 seconds; halt through gradual transitions through trot and walk and take the rates. Finally, walk for 10 minutes and take them again.

Once again, you can build up the times until you are cantering for 3 minutes, trotting for 3 minutes, cantering for another 3 minutes and returning to halt to check heart and respiration rates. As always, carry out your final 10-minute walk period and check the rates once more.

As your horse finds it easier to recover and his rates become more stable, so he will find the work easier. You can then either increase the length of the canter periods, or build up to three, 3-minute canters. If you want to build his fitness further, you can then move up to the stronger canter estimated earlier, covering 400 m (440 yards) per minute. Start with two canter periods and when his recovery rates indicate that he is coping well, add a third.

Chapter **Seven**

Schooling

E VERY HORSE SHOULD BE A responsive, balanced, obedient ride who is
happy to work for and with his rider. In other words, he needs to be
well schooled and willing. If he isn't willing, he won't be happy to go
forward; if he isn't balanced, he won't be able to carry himself correctly and
if he isn't obedient, you're not in control!

At any dressage competition, you'll see lots of horses who can do more or
less what is required but do not present a picture of overall harmony –
usually because they are forced into an outline rather than having been
helped to develop it through correct and sympathetic work. Any horse, no
matter what his breed or type, even though he may be restricted in some
respects by the limits of his conformation, can be schooled to become an
enjoyable, rewarding ride. To put this point more into perspective, the
restrictions may not matter one iota to most riders, as few of us aim to ride
at the highest levels of affiliated competition.

Watch any horse out in the field, whether he is a Warmblood bred for
dressage through countless generations or a cob or heavy horse, and you'll
see times when he displays an amazing athleticism. Heavy horses can and do
float over the ground when they are full of the joys of life, showing elevation
in their movement that most of us would give our eye teeth to be able to
obtain under saddle. However, when they are asked to carry a rider, it puts a
burden on them in more senses than the literal one.

A horse's back may look as if it is designed to carry weight, and to some
extent, it is, as his internal organs are supported by soft tissue connected to
the spine and the ribs. But add the weight of a saddle and rider and you are
adding stresses the back is not designed to take. In response to this, the horse's

7.1 and **7.2** Even horses who don't immediately strike you as dressage material can be schooled to go correctly – and may surprise you with their talent!

natural reaction is to lift his head and neck, whilst the back dips very slightly and the hind legs are put further behind than when he moves unencumbered.

To enable him to work in the way we want – and which, when he is physically capable of doing it, is the most efficient way – he has to be able to lift his abdominal muscles, which in turn will mean that he raises his back slightly, lowers his head and places his hind legs more underneath his body. This posture also means that he is more likely to accept the bit happily, as it won't be pulling down on the bars of his mouth, as happens when he raises his head, and the rider is less likely to try to 'niggle' or even pull him into a perceived outline.

To achieve this to the extent where the horse can work on the bit for long periods takes time, as the horse doesn't have the muscular development to hold such a posture. A lungeing programme such as that outlined in Chapter 2 helps to start this process. For most riders, getting a horse to work on the bit is the Holy Grail of schooling, which often means they become obsessed with getting him to arch his neck and work in a 'round outline'. Often without realising it, they concentrate so much on getting this that they end up restricting the horse in front, setting up tension throughout his body and forgetting that the horse must be going forward and working from behind.

A horse may need to learn to compensate for what nature didn't provide. There are some whose conformation means they are naturally 'born on the bit' – though their natural advantages can still be lost by bad riding or incorrect schooling – but there are many more who aren't. For instance, many heavier horses and cobs have less space between their jawbones than is ideal, and also have a V-shaped angle to the throat rather than a rounded one (see

7.3 *left* When a horse can take the correct posture, he will be more likely to accept the bit happily.

7.4 *below* If a horse has a V-shaped angle to the throat rather than a rounded one, it is harder for him to flex.

photo 7.4.) This makes it harder for them to flex and, in some cases, their breathing may be restricted when they are asked to work in a round outline to the extent that you will hear them making a noise. Similarly, a horse whose neck comes out of the withers relatively low, as is the case with most Thoroughbreds, will often feel naturally 'downhill' until he has learned to lift from underneath and starts to develop muscle along the top of his neck.

Horses who are being asked to move in an outline they have not been prepared for through consistent work not surprisingly find it difficult. They often show this through resistance, which can be manifest in a variety of ways and in varying degrees. The commonest is tension, which can affect the horse from head to tail – he may be tight through his neck and back, stiffen through his jaw, swish his tail rather than let it swing from side to side in a relaxed way, come above or behind the bit for long periods, snatch at the reins or show other resistances in his mouth.

Mouth resistances are also common in horses whose riders try to enforce an outline through the reins. What often happens next is that the rider

Bring out the **BEST IN YOUR HORSE**

decides to fasten the horse's mouth shut with a tight noseband – which, in turn, leads to yet more resistance and tension. Alternatively, a rider may decide that the best approach is to work a horse without any rein contact, in the hope that everything will suddenly and miraculously fall into place. Whilst this probably doesn't do any harm – and certainly causes far fewer problems than if the reins are used to try to force a horse to adopt a particular outline – it isn't productive, either.

At one time, 'making a horse's mouth' was a key part of the breaking – or starting, if you prefer the term – process. Now, it seems to be given little consideration by some trainers and riders. That's a pity, because teaching a horse to accept and respond to light signals on the bit can be done even before he is ridden, as explained later. Not only is it the kindest and most logical way to educate a young horse, it can also be used to overcome problems in an older horse.

Another question you have to ask is whether you are causing or contributing to the fact that your horse doesn't go as well as you'd like him to. The answer is almost certainly yes, because any imbalance in a rider is reflected by imbalance in the horse. Sometimes, horse and rider compound each other's problems: for instance, a horse who falls in on the right rein may drop the rider's weight to the inside so that he falls in even further. If you don't realise what's happening, it may feel as if you're sitting centrally when you're actually lopsided.

Outside help from the right teacher – or even from a friend who can tell you if what you're feeling is what's actually happening – is essential. That's why even Olympic riders get help! If you school on your own most of the time, you can also tend to develop a negative approach to your horse's work. It's essential to realise what needs improving, but solo schooling often leads to a mindset where you only notice the minus points and not the plus, simply because you're riding the horse every day. It's only when someone points out that a horse is actually finding work easier than he did a couple of months ago, or points out that, perhaps, his canter transitions are much smoother and in balance, that you realise you are making an improvement.

Also, someone who works with different types of horses and riders should build a wide range of tactics and exercises to help you overcome problems. There are lots of great books, magazines, websites and DVDs that will give you inspiration, some of which are listed at the end of this book, but the ultimate secret weapon is a teacher you can relate to, and who relates to you and your horse, and who can help you progress. Finding the right teacher isn't always easy; whilst we all need to be encouraged to improve, personalities and approaches come into it.

7.5 Outside help from a good trainer will help you and your horse improve – and will also give you vital encouragement.

Hopefully, the days of the instructor who shouts at pupils until they're too frightened to move is over, but at the opposite end of the scale, you don't want someone who tells you you're wonderful all the time. You also need to make sure that your trainer helps you develop and achieve goals, whether these be competing or hacking out safely and enjoyably. Competing isn't everything, though a lot of riders find it's a good yardstick for measuring how their training is progressing, but both you and your horse will enjoy working towards challenges.

As the broad scope of this book makes it impractical to give a detailed guide to schooling and riding techniques, this chapter is meant to remind you of things you may have taken for granted or forgotten and to give ideas of ways to bring about an improvement. It isn't meant to be a guide on how to produce a competition dressage horse, but simply how to make sure your horse is a pleasure to ride and that, whether you are working him in a school or going for a hack, starting from scratch with an unbacked horse or dealing with a more established one, your relationship is a happy and confident one.

Starting out

If you've bought this book because you're lucky enough to have a young horse and the chance to give him a good start in life, you may be wondering what is the best way to do it. These days, economic pressure means that many horses are backed and expected to work in walk, trot and canter in a space of four to six weeks. This is especially true when they are sent by their owners to a professional training yard, as the bills soon add up. Ideally, every horse should be allowed to progress at his own pace; in practice, some owners can't afford to do this.

Starting a young horse's education is a big responsibility and it's understandable that many owners feel they don't have the necessary expertise. However, that can lead to a chicken and egg situation, as everyone has to start somewhere! A lot of backing and riding away is down to common sense, patience and confidence. There's no place for bravado, because that's when accidents happen, and it isn't something that nervous riders should undertake, because they will transmit their nervousness to the horse.

Only you can decide the right way to do things, but if you have a young horse you know well and who has shown confidence in all you have done with him so far, you may want to consider whether you can start him off yourself. Horses are remarkably accepting and trusting and if he's never had any bad experiences, and you do your best to ensure that continues by giving him time to accept every new step, you could find it a rewarding experience and a definite learning curve.

There are, of course, outside factors that may mean this isn't feasible. You need someone sensible to help you and you also need safe surroundings in which to work him. Whilst you don't need to be able to work with him every day, you do need to be sure that when you introduce a new experience, you have as long as it takes for him to be confident and happy.

Some people may be surprised by the belief that you don't need to work a youngster every day. It's purely a personal opinion and may not apply to some horses – but I've often found that introducing a horse to a new experience over a few days, then giving him a day or two to absorb it before going on to the next step, pays dividends. It means there's no danger of subjecting the horse to mental overload and you'll find that once he accepts something for the first time, he should accept it equally happily next time round. Obviously you have to take the horse's temperament into account and it's also important to start your next session with a lesson he has already mastered, then move on to the new one.

Some horses and ponies have temperaments which make them unsuitable for most first-time trainers. A horse who is nervous or particularly sharp to react needs a trainer who is sympathetic, but used to dealing with young horses of different types and able to assess how to give him confidence. You have to accept that whilst a sharp horse will often become less reactive as he gains experience, that only comes through time – and the speed of his reactions will probably always demand a rider who can not only give an equally fast response, but keep a split second ahead of him.

If you have a young horse and think he may be a bit of a challenge, but you also have plenty of time to start his education, it may be worth buying a potentially easier youngster with whom to gain experience first. The term 'project horse' is often seen in adverts now and is usually a euphemism for an animal with problems, but there can be projects of a different kind. As long as you are prepared to take responsibility for eventually finding him a suitable home, it can be very rewarding to buy a pony or horse with an easy-going temperament and gain experience and confidence by working with him, ideally with a trainer you can call on for advice if there's anything you're not sure about.

You will make mistakes and experience setbacks – but you'll do that with every subsequent horse you take on. The commonest scenario is when a horse has been so chilled in his response to new experiences that you take it for granted that he will accept everything with equanimity, only to find something small and silly that frightens him.

There are many different approaches to backing a horse, ranging from the traditional, structured approach that starts with lungeing and long-reining and progresses through the actual backing process and riding on the lunge to riding loose, to systems popularised by celebrity trainers. Although many of the latter are talented and instinctive horse people, the marketing and hype that surrounds some of their demonstrations sadly doesn't always present their expertise in the best light: sometimes, the main focus seems to be on how quickly they can get on a previously unridden horse.

Ideally, we can take inspiration from many different approaches. Some of the key points to think about when backing your own horse are:

- Don't get fixated on time. 'It takes as long as it takes' is a great motto. Horses, like children, don't learn at the same rate. In the same way, they may find some things easy and others more difficult, or more worrying. It doesn't mean that one horse is more or less intelligent than another, just that you have to give each one time to be confident with each stage.

- It's also useful to be able to give a horse a little break when he's taken in a lot of new information. Although it may sound silly, horses really do assimilate things and if you teach him to, say, lunge and long-rein, then give him two or three days off and start again, you'll often find that he is more confident. It sometimes seems as if he's been thinking about something and the penny has dropped, but it's more likely to be that he's had a chance to relax after a lot of new experiences.

- Instilling good behaviour on the ground will help your horse to work with you under saddle; traditional trainers have always known this, but it has perhaps taken modern ones to really get the message across. However, the fact that you can get your horse to 'join up' or move away from pressure on a halter does not mean that you can get straight on him and expect him to understand how to stop, start and steer! Similarly, backing a horse – in the context of getting him to accept a rider on his back and walking and trotting round an enclosed area – does not mean that he is broken in, or started, if you prefer the latter term. It is only the first step in his education; backing a horse is a bit like learning a few basic phrases in a new language. To become fluent takes more time, education and practice.

- Break every new experience into small steps. For instance, when you're grooming a young horse, get him used to you standing on a small, safe mounting block so that you are standing above him as you work. To get him used to the idea of something round his belly, hold a stretch tail bandage round his middle and tighten it gently, then hold it whilst a helper moves him round the stable. If he hasn't worn rugs, introduce them calmly and correctly; again, this helps to introduce the idea of something on his back.

- Introduce a bit carefully and teach him to accept it and to understand basic signals from the ground – see next section. The fact that a horse stays calm about wearing a bit in his mouth does not mean that he will automatically understand rein signals – and, of course, you want these to be minimal. If you pull at a horse's mouth you will confuse him and cause him discomfort. Depending on his temperament, he will either pull back or run off in panic.

- Whilst many trainers use a bit from the start, with great results, it is well worth thinking about carrying out early riding using nose pressure alone. Although this has been claimed as a new idea by some trainers, it is a practice that – according to the late author and authority on saddlery Elwyn Harley Edwards – goes back to the seventh century, during the Moorish occupation of the Iberian Peninsula, when horsemen used a heavy rawhide noseband with a rear knot and a rope rein to teach the horse to turn to subtle signals, including shifts in the rider's weight.

Making the mouth

Nothing is nicer than riding a horse who accepts the bit confidently and is soft and responsive to subtle rein aids. Sadly, this isn't always the case and many horses are unresponsive or resistant. As explained earlier, mouth resistances are not necessarily linked to mouth problems – they may be a symptom of tension or discomfort elsewhere in the horse's body – but many are down to the fact that horses have not been correctly introduced to a bit and taught to respond to its signals.

At one time, 'making a horse's mouth' was a traditional nagsman's skill and trainers would spend days or weeks laying the foundations for a horse's future, whether that was to be riding or driving. There are still trainers who realise the importance of this, but a combination of economic pressure and time restrictions during the breaking process and some riders' lack of appreciation of how important this process is results in many horses who learn to respond to the bit by trial and error. The problems with such an approach are that communication errors are inevitable and horses 'tune out' to subtle signals. A similar situation can happen with a horse's reaction to leg and seat aids, as explained in the next section. Fortunately, both can be improved.

People often talk about horse having a soft mouth or a hard mouth, but these terms really refer to response rather than to physical characteristics. It is sometimes said that a horse with a high percentage of Thoroughbred blood has a thinner layer of skin over the bars of the mouth, where the bit rests, which in turn supposedly makes him more sensitive than a cold-blooded horse – a bit like the old fairy tale of the princess and the pea, where only the true blue-blooded princess could feel the pea placed under her mattress. However, it's debatable whether there is such a difference. Also, when a horse seems to 'harden' his mouth, he may actually be showing resistance in his neck and body. Asking him to soften through his neck should result in a softer response through his mouth as, when he relaxes his neck, you should also find that he relaxes his jaw.

Stage 1

If you are introducing a bit as part of the breaking process, your first task is to get the horse to accept and be comfortable with what, to him, is a foreign object in his mouth. Different trainers have different ideas about the best way to do this – but in my experience, starting with a lightweight, unjointed plastic mouthpiece that is not too thick (see photo 7.6) often gets good results. With many horses, you can also use these to start their ridden education, though you may need to change to different designs if you require more definite signals later on. You also have to accept that even high-tech materials cannot withstand a horse's teeth and although these bits should have a central core, they won't last forever.

7.6 A bit with a lightweight, unjointed plastic mouthpiece is often a good first choice for a young horse.

Some people like to smear a mouthpiece with honey or molasses to encourage the horse to accept it, but it's more important to introduce a bridle sympathetically. Remove the noseband and reins and start by getting the horse used to having the headpiece, minus bit, passed over his ears; if you've accustomed him to having his ears handled, this shouldn't be a problem.

Next, attach the bit and let the horse investigate it – nine times out of ten, he'll explore it with his mouth and you can gently slip it in and pass the headpiece over his ears, as before. Some horses accept a bit straight away whilst others pull faces and try to spit it out. Make sure it's high enough in the mouth to be difficult for him to put his tongue over it, but not so high that it pulls his lips into a false smile. This is another advantage of an unjointed mouthpiece, as it naturally sits higher in the mouth.

Leave the horse in the stable with his bit in for a few minutes, having taken out any mangers or buckets, but stay with him to make sure he doesn't rub his face against anything he could get the bit rings hooked up on. After a few minutes, remove the bridle with equal care. Repeat for a few days, gradually increasing the time until he is happy to wear a bit for half an hour at a time. Always make sure you are within earshot during these sessions and are close enough to reach him immediately if there is a problem.

Occasionally, you'll get a horse or pony who is so cross at having to wear something in his mouth that he'll spend all his time trying to get rid of it, crossing his jaw and sticking his tongue out. In this case, it's often best to give him something to think about so he doesn't fixate on trying to get rid of the bit. Fit a coupling that fastens to the noseband as well as to the bit rings, as explained further in Stage 3, and introduce the idea of walking and halting in a safe, enclosed area. Use your voice and make light signals that are distinctly 'on' and 'off' rather than applying prolonged pressure.

Some trainers will lead a horse directly from the bit right from the start, but the advantage of using a coupling is that pressure is divided between the nose – a signal he is already familiar with through being led in a headcollar – and the mouth. It also means that you are not putting more pressure on one side of the mouth than the other; obviously that will come later, as you introduce steering, but at the moment, you are concentrating on the basic 'stop' and 'go'.

Stage 2

Once your horse is happy wearing a bit, you may like to introduce side reins as his first experience of a slight weight on the bit. They must be adjusted loosely, as you are not trying to establish a contact. As a guide, work out how long they would be if there were to be the lightest contact when the horse stands with his nose just in front of the vertical, then lengthen them by a further five or six holes.

There are pros and cons to this practice. The advantage is that the horse teaches himself that a gentle feel on the mouth is nothing to worry about; the disadvantage is that some horses have a bit of a tantrum at the slightest hint of restriction and throw their heads around, pulling themselves in the mouth. On balance, the pros tend to outweigh the cons – it's probably better for the horse to throw a strop at this stage than with a rider, and as you're using the mildest possible bit, the horse is not going to be hurt. Once he is happy to accept and perhaps mouth a little on the bit, you can shorten the side reins by a couple of holes.

This stage is also useful when you are trying to improve an experienced horse's sensitivity to the bit, as many simply don't understand that if they give to slight pressure, it immediately releases – and so the horse rewards himself. Although it's worth starting with a simple plastic mouthpiece when working with an older horse, you may find that a metal one designed to encourage the horse to salivate is more effective, as explained in Chapter 4.

Stage 3

The next stage is to teach your horse to respond to gentle pressure on the reins. If you are backing a horse and he already understands verbal commands to walk on and halt, use a snaffle bridle with a cavesson noseband, your snaffle bit of choice and a coupling which disperses pressure over the nose and mouth – these are usually used for showing youngsters in hand.

7.7 A coupling disperses pressure over the nose and mouth and means you are not putting more pressure on one side of the bit than the other.

The lead rein or rope fastens to the central ring, so you are not putting more pressure on one side of the mouth than the other.

Lead your horse in a safe, enclosed area and practise simple walk to halt transitions, using the voice command, your body language and an 'on and off' signal on the lead rein at the same time. If you have already taught him this as part of instilling manners on the ground (see Chapter 5) he should quickly realise what you want. Don't set up a consistent pull, as it's important that as soon as the horse obeys, the pressure is released. If he doesn't obey, ask again until he's got the message.

When this is established, you can repeat the lesson leading him directly from the bit, and then teach him to flex at the poll and relax his jaw. He should already be used to doing this on a headcollar or halter, so asking him via the bit is a natural extension. To keep it simple, stand at the side of your horse with the reins loose on his neck. Although we should try and handle horses equally from both sides, we inevitably do more from the left than the right, and as many horses find it easier to bend this way, it makes sense to start by standing on the left-hand side.

Stand at his left side and hold the reins under his neck, with your hands about 18 cm (7 in) from the bit. Keeping a light contact on the right rein, squeeze gently with your fingers on the left (see photo 7.8). If he responds by flexing to the left and lowering his head, however slight the movement, relax the reins. If you don't get a response, ask again. Eventually, the penny will

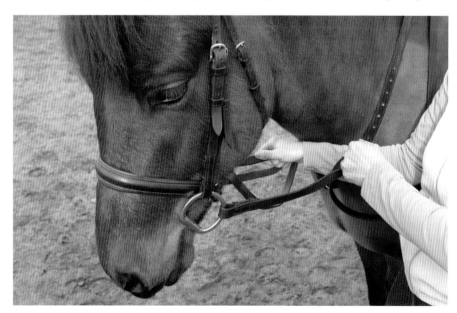

7.8 You can introduce the concept of bending and flexing through in-hand work.

drop. As always, repeat on the other side, this time keeping a light contact on the left rein and squeezing on the right.

Working in hand like this will only introduce the idea of responding to pressure, flexing and bending. As already discussed, a horse can only work in self-carriage and be light and responsive to the aids when he has the correct build-up of muscles and works from behind. This is something that he learns over a long period of time – and, of course, all the other building blocks, including a balanced rider, have to be in place.

Ridden basics

It's often said that schooling a horse is like building a pyramid, in that the foundation has to be secure to save things getting shaky as you go up the levels. With riding, the classical basics are that the horse is calm, forward and straight – and yes, it can be easy to forget them.

A calm horse is one who accepts what the rider asks him to do and responds without resistance or tension. Inevitably, there will be times when you get breakdowns in communication, but hopefully these will be short and quickly remedied. There will also be times when a horse is excited or just a bit full of himself, perhaps because it's a windy day or he's simply full of the joy of life.

These situations don't become problems unless they are happening too often, in which case you need to look at possible reasons. Are you confusing him with your aids or asking him questions more complicated than he can understand? Is he getting too much high-energy food and not enough time out in the field?

The horse who always seems to be tense, resentful or nervous is a different matter. There can be so many causes, from discomfort to the horse being put under permanent pressure by his rider, that you need to be able to find out whether he has a soundness problem, ascertain his state of mind and assess how you keep and ride him. It's often said that all a horse has to do in return for a comfortable life is go nicely for an hour each day, but it isn't quite as simple as that. Horses, like people, need a work/life balance: they need enough training/schooling to be safe, pleasurable rides, but within that discipline they need variety and opportunities to relax.

Calmness doesn't mean laziness or that the horse is 'switched off.' A horse just starting out on his education will need more time to understand and react to your aids, but although they need to be clear, you shouldn't get into a situation with any horse where you are kicking and/or pulling.

A horse needs to be 'forward' so that, in basic terms, he responds to your aids *to do anything* immediately. You also want to ensure that you aren't working harder than he is! It's often said that a horse should be 'in front of the leg', a rather strange phrase that means he is willing to go forward as soon as he is asked; however, he should be as willing to go forward to a slower gait as to a faster one. This applies whether you are working on the flat or jumping.

It isn't as Alice in Wonderland-ish as it first sounds to talk about going forward to a slower gait/going forward into a downward transition. It means that the horse stays active from behind and in balance, rather than falling on to his forehand and grinding down into a lower gear. The more established and better-schooled a horse is, the easier this becomes for him and the more subtle the riders' signals can be. For instance, for a horse in the early stages of schooling, going from canter to walk will mean progressing through trot, whilst a horse who is much more advanced in his education will be able to go from canter to walk or canter to halt.

It's also important to understand what is *not* meant by going forward. A horse who is rushing or pulling isn't 'forward' in the true sense of the term; just like the lazy horse, he isn't responding to your aids.

7.9 and **7.10** A horse should respond to your aids immediately, whether on the flat or when jumping, so he goes forward and comes back to you as soon as you ask.

Another phrase worth remembering is that a horse should 'accept the leg' and not be frightened of it. Most young horses, if they are backed correctly, accept leg and weight aids because they are taught to associate them with the verbal commands used when they are lungeing and long-reining. However, if a horse is rushed or frightened, he may associate a rider's weight and the

contact of the rider's legs on his sides with a worrying experience and need to be taken right back to square one.

Lazy or unresponsive horses

The most common problem is the horse who is thought of as lazy or unresponsive. In most cases, this is the result of him switching off, either to his rider's aids, his work regime, or both. The answer, once you've ruled out obvious causes relating to health and discomfort, is often to do less, but make what you do more effective. It's easy to get into the habit of continually using your legs and, in doing so, you get into a vicious cycle: the horse switches off and ignores your signals, so you carry on giving them and end up nagging at him.

If you're in this situation and you've checked that your horse is sound, free from discomfort and neither overweight nor undernourished – the former being far more common – you need to teach him that going forward is easier and more pleasant than being recalcitrant. Some people may advise riding him in spurs, but this is not generally recommended: spurs are used to refine aids, not as extra accelerators.

Start by teaching him to go forward on the ground, ideally using a control headcollar such as a Dually, a long lead rope and a schooling whip. Stand at or just in front of his shoulder, look to the front and give a sharp click with your tongue as you step forward. Hopefully, he will walk on immediately. If he doesn't, or if he's slow to respond, halt, click again and if there is no immediate response, flick the schooling whip against his side.

If he jumps forward, go with him – it's crucial not to ask him to go forwards, but then pull back when he obeys. If his response is still sluggish, repeat the process and upgrade the flick of the whip to a sharp tap. Nine times out of ten, this will work and you can praise the horse. Once he's got the idea, you can decrease the stimulus until he responds to a click.

You can now transfer what he's learned on the ground to work under saddle. Although it's been said so often it has become a cliché, a horse is sensitive enough to feel a fly land on his side, so there is no reason why he can't be taught to respond to a light leg aid. The first step is to check that you are using your leg in the right place and not blocking with your body language at the same time – when you get frustrated, it's easy to become tense without realising it and when this happens, your legs might be saying 'Go' but your body will be saying 'Stop!' An effective rider is toned, but not tense, with strong core muscles that allow him or her to maintain a balanced position without relying on reins or stirrups.

The right place to use your legs is often referred to as being 'on the girth', but is really *very slightly* behind it, since this area has a lot of nerve endings and is highly sensitive. That said, a lot of riders use their legs *too far* back. This will be less effective and may also tip your body weight forwards. If you find it difficult to use your legs in the correct place, check that the design of your saddle and in particular, the placement of the stirrup bars, is not hindering rather than helping you (see Chapter 4). A training aid for riders called Symmetry lower leg training straps, from Equilibrium Products, might help. These attach the stirrup leathers to the girth and help give the idea of a correct lower leg position, though there is a breakaway action for safety.

7.11 These Symmetry lower leg training straps can be a useful rider training aid.

To ask your horse to go forward, look ahead and think forward. It may sound silly, but if you are purposeful in your attitude, your horse will pick up on the subtle messages through your posture. Use your calves in a gentle, forward 'on and off' movement and if he responds, don't keep repeating the aid. If you don't get a response, add the click and if necessary, use the schooling whip as before. Make sure you don't restrict him as he goes forward and don't nag with your legs as he does so: use your aids if he loses his forward momentum and let your legs rest round his side without applying pressure whilst he maintains it.

Horses who don't respond to a schooling whip may react better to a wip-wop or over-and-under. This can be made simply from an old head-collar rope; remove the clip and tie a loop with which to hold it. To use a wip-wop, hold it in one hand and the reins loosely in the other, to avoid catching the horse in the mouth. If the horse does not respond to a light leg aid, flip the wip-wop from one side to the other so it goes over his withers and your leg (see photos 7.12 and 7.13). You aren't hitting the horse and, in many cases, may not even have to touch him – the sight of the rope moving will prompt forward movement. Because he may shoot forward at first, make sure you are in safe surroundings. It's also a good idea to use a neckstrap in case you need help keeping your balance.

Is your horse lazy all the time, or just in a schooling situation? Whilst he has to learn to respond to you all the time, some horses switch off in a schooling session, often because they aren't given enough variety. Endless going round in circles is as boring for a horse or pony as it is for his rider, so find ways to keep him thinking. Ride lots of transitions and make variations within the gaits, shortening and lengthening the stride; use poles on the

7.12 and **7.13** Some horses may respond better to a wip-wop (over-and-under) than to a schooling whip as an encouragement to go forward.

ground and small jumps; ride figures that incorporate lots of changes of direction and gait.

Just as importantly, don't forget that you can school on a hack as well as in an arena and, in many cases, you'll find that because your horse is more inclined to go forwards, you'll get better results. Once he's got the message that quick responses make life easier for him, you'll find it easier to reproduce this way of going in a school. See Chapter 8 for more ideas.

Horses who rush

The problem of the older horse who rushes is sometimes harder to resolve and requires a rider who can remain calm and balanced and be relied on not to pull at the horse's mouth in an attempt to slow him down. That doesn't mean that he should be ridden on a loose rein all the time, though some loose rein work will help.

If the horse rushes because he anticipates being socked in the teeth, you need to give him confidence in the reins. One of the best ways to do this is by lungeing him in a mild snaffle with side reins attached, introducing them as explained in Chapter 2. Lunge him from the centre ring of a cavesson rather than with the lunge rein over his head to avoid pressure on the bit and, if necessary, get help from someone who is experienced in lungeing different sorts of horses.

7.14 A 'pull and release' on a neckstrap can encourage a horse who rushes to slow down and rebalance himself.

Ridden work should be restricted to walk until the horse starts to gain confidence, so make sure he's out as much as possible and in most cases, keep to a forage-only diet. Fit a neckstrap and use this and your weight aids to ask him to go from walk to halt – sit tall, consciously stop following the movement of his body with your own and close your fingers on the reins without pulling back. If this doesn't work, slip your fingers under the neckstrap and give a short pull and release.

When he's got the idea, which may take more than one session, quietly ask for trot. Try to keep a light contact on the reins and if your horse starts to rush, use lots of turns and changes of direction to help keep him thinking. If you find yourself tightening your arm muscles – and don't beat yourself up if you do, because it's a natural reaction for most people when a horse goes faster than they want him to – try reins which incorporate an elastic section or hold the reins upside down, with thumbs on top, as if you were holding a pair of frying pans. This releases tension in your arm muscles and, when you return to your usual position, you'll remember the correct feel.

Stay in rising trot and slow your rise, which usually means your horse will slow his trot to mirror your movement. As before, use your weight aids and neckstrap to ask for transitions to walk and if your horse wants to, let him stretch his head and neck down, as this is a sign that he is starting to relax.

You won't turn your horse from a Duracell bunny into a calm, relaxed ride overnight – or even in a week – but with patience, you will make

7.15 Holding one or both reins 'upside down' will prevent tension in your arm muscles.

progress. However, you will have to allow yourself to be a calming influence, by staying relaxed – in a toned rather than a floppy or slumping way. Exercises to release tension whilst establishing and maintaining core stability will help enormously. Pilates is great for anyone and absolutely wonderful for riders (see Last Word at the end of this book).

Straightness

The final part of this basic schooling triangle, which underlines the work of every horse, is to ensure that he is straight – which is a lot easier said than done. Even the most brilliant riders on horses they have spent years schooling towards perfection will deviate from straightness, if only for a split second at a time. Horses, like people, are usually one-sided and though most horses find it easier to work on one rein than the other, it's obvious that when a rider uses stronger aids with one side of the body than the other, it will affect the horse's way of going. That's why it's important to get an MoT for yourself every now and again and to try to compensate for the stresses and strains everyday life imposes (see Last Word).

Although it may sound rather Double Dutch, a horse has to be able to bend equally on both reins before he can be straight and he has to be 'straight' on turns and circles as well as on a straight line – his hindquarters should not swing in or out and, except when he is doing lateral work, his hind feet should follow the same tracks as his forefeet. The best definition I have found of how this relates to lateral work comes from *The Allen Illustrated Encyclopaedia of Dressage*, compiled by Martin Diggle (J.A. Allen): 'When a horse is performing lateral movements, a quality of movement equating to straightness is evidenced by the feet moving consistently on lines that are parallel and spaced appropriately according to the exercise being performed and the angle of travel required.'

The horse's natural crookedness aside, the commonest reason for lack of straightness on turns and circles is that the rider uses too much inside rein to try to produce the desired bend. What happens then is that the horse's forward movement is restricted and the horse can't bring his inside hind leg beneath him. Direct use of the inside rein will only bend the head and neck; to ask the horse to bend through his body, you have to use your inside leg, with your outside leg slightly back to prevent his hindquarters swinging out, whilst the inside hand opens the rein slightly to ask the horse to look and flex in the direction of the turn and the outside rein contains the shoulder and stops it falling to the outside. It's important that you open the rein to the side without pulling back.

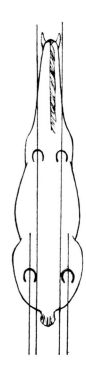

7.16 Illustration of straightness, originally from *Dressage as Art in Competition*, reproduced in *The Allen Illustrated Encyclopaedia of Dressage*.

Forward and sideways

Lateral work, where the horse is asked to move forwards and sideways at the same time, and at an angle appropriate to the level of his schooling, helps to keep him straight. This might sound topsy turvy, but lateral work will help you keep your horse on the outside aids rather than trying to straighten him with the inside rein, as explained above. It can be introduced very early on in the horse's education.

The most useful exercises to help straightness are shoulder-in and leg-yielding. Although some lateral work requires that the horse is able to work in collection, this isn't necessary for the first stages of either exercise.

Shoulder-in

Shoulder-in encourages the horse to step under with his inside hind leg and bend through his body. His inside foreleg crosses in front of the outside one and the inside hind leg steps forwards and across. If you watch a horse performing true shoulder-in correctly, at an angle of about 30 degrees, then from the front you should see that the inside hind leg is in line with the outside foreleg.

It's too much to expect a horse to manage this angle and maintain forward momentum right from the start. Instead, ask for a much shallower

7.17 A good example of shoulder-fore or 'position-in', which is the first stage of achieving shoulder-in.

angle; when the exercise is ridden this way it is often called 'position-in' or shoulder-fore, as shown in photo 7.17. The easiest way to teach it is to walk a 15-m circle, starting from a point on the long side of the school, just past the first quarter marker. As you complete the circle and rejoin the long side, allow an initial step as though you were riding a second circle, then use your inside leg to ask the horse to step off the line of the circle and down the line of the long side.

What you have done is used the circle to produce a bend in the horse's body, then asked him to maintain that shape but take it off the circle on to a straight track parallel with the school perimeter.

The main aid comes from the inside leg, but you should keep your outside leg slightly behind the girth (where it was on the circle) to prevent the horse from straightening his quarters and you can bring your outside hand to the base of his neck to encourage his shoulders to stay over (don't use this hand to try to 'drag' him down the long side). Don't ask for too much, too soon – be content with two or three steps, then straighten the horse. Once your horse is performing this exercise happily and correctly in walk, ask him to perform it in trot; this asks for greater activity and engagement of the inside hind leg.

Turn on the forehand and leg-yielding

Leg-yielding, where the horse moves forward and sideways with just a small amount of neck flexion away from the direction of movement, also helps with engagement and suppleness. Many trainers like to teach turn on the forehand as an introduction to this exercise – if you do this first from the ground, as discussed in Chapter 5, the progression is even easier.

For turn on the forehand, the horse is ridden forwards to a square halt, then asked to move his back end over, pivoting on his inside foreleg and crossing his inside hind leg in front of the outside one. The direction of the movement is defined by the front end, not the back – so in a turn on the forehand to the right, the horse will be flexed slightly right and his back end will move to the left. The rider's right leg will be inside leg and the left leg, the outside one.

It's useful to have a helper on the ground when you first introduce the idea. If necessary, the helper can nudge the horse over whilst the rider gives the leg aids and, if he misunderstands and moves forward, indicates with the outside rein that this isn't want is wanted. Some horses take a little while to understand that the leg aid in this use doesn't mean 'Go forward'; if yours is one of them, don't pull back on the rein or he may become agitated. It's better to let him take a step forward and then move over as, once he can manage this calmly, he should respond better when asked to go sideways but not forward.

Ask for one step at a time to start with, using your leg in an on and off nudge rather than applying constant pressure. Some trainers believe that the leg should be used behind the girth, but others prefer to use it on the girth. Most horses seem to respond well if you use your leg very slightly behind the girth. As soon as he steps over, reward him and ride forward. As he starts to find it easier you can introduce more steps – but always ride forward afterwards and don't be too ambitious in the number of steps you ask for, or you'll lose the essential momentum.

Turn on the forehand is an exercise that sometimes shows one-sidedness very clearly. Some horses, in the early days of this movement, may 'get it' immediately when asked to turn one way, and really struggle (and perhaps resist) when asked to turn the other way. If your horse is willing to do it in one direction, it is unlikely that he resists in the other direction out of sheer cussedness; take this on board and compare his different responses to how he works on both reins in other movements.

In leg-yielding, the horse moves forward and sideways, with just a small amount of flexion in his neck away from the direction of the movement – so if he is going forward and sideways to the left, his neck will be flexed slightly right. The commonest mistake is to ask for too much flexion; if this happens, you'll often get better results by just thinking about it, rather than using the inside rein. What will happen then is that you'll automatically adjust your weight, though you'll need to keep a contact on the outside rein. Make sure you understand what the terms inside and outside mean with reference to the rider: they refer to the way the horse is bent, so in this example, your right leg and hand would be the inside ones.

The easiest way to introduce leg-yielding is from the three-quarter line of the school. In walk, ride straight for two or three strides, then ask for or think about flexion to the inside whilst keeping your horse forward and straight, with your outside leg very slightly behind the girth. Nudge him on or slightly behind the girth with your inside leg and his natural inclination to go back to the track should get the desired response. It might be wobbly, but at this stage, that doesn't matter. Once the horse understands the aids, ride the exercise from the track into the school to make sure he is working correctly and that you and he are not using the track as a 'safety blanket' or 'magnet'.

Once he can perform this exercise on both reins – and he'll probably find it easier on one than the other – try leg-yielding in trot. Because you'll have more forward momentum, this should help straighten out any wobbles; however, introducing it in walk gives both of you more time to think about what you're doing. As with shoulder-in, quality means more than quantity and it's better to get two good steps of leg-yielding and ride forwards than to try and hold it for more strides than your horse can comfortably manage at that stage.

There are lots of useful exercises in which you can incorporate leg-yielding. One which really helps to reinforce the outside aids is to ride a 20-m circle, spiral down to 15 m and leg-yield back out to 20 m. As your horse becomes more advanced, you can ride a leg-yield zigzag. Ride straight down the centre line, then leg-yield out for two or three strides, ride straight for two strides and then leg-yield back to the centre line. Repeat until you are nearly at the end of the school, ride a 10-m half-circle to bring you back on the centre line and repeat.

Poles and grid work

7.18 Be content with a couple of good steps of leg-yielding to start with.

Even if you don't want to jump routinely, working over poles on the ground and through simple grids can be of enormous benefit to your horse's way of going and will also help keep him (and perhaps you) interested in schooling work. Riders who don't want to leave the ground at all should not forget the value of poles on the ground, for the same reasons – remember the box of poles exercise from Chapter 2.

For the sake of safety, and also because it's a nuisance if you have to keep getting off to adjust poles, always have a helper when you're jumping. It's also useful to have someone who can alter the distances between poles on the ground. Some riders prefer to use planks rather than round poles, as the former are more likely to stay in place.

There are lots of specialist grids and exercises that can be built to help solve particular problems, but a few tried and tested examples are listed below for everyday use. Where striding distances are given, they are for an average horse's stride, so you'll need to reduce them for ponies. If your horse has a particularly long stride, you can lengthen them a little.

Canter poles on a circle

Place four poles on the ground so their centres mark the quarters of the circumference of a 20-m circle – if you imagine your circle is a clock face, the poles will be at 12, 3, 6 and 9 o'clock. First trot over the poles, then canter, aiming to keep the same rhythm and meet each pole on a normal stride. If your horse loses his rhythm and falls into trot, ask him to strike off into canter as you go over the next pole. Work equally on both reins.

A variation on this exercise will help a more experienced horse establish a forward but controlled canter and encourage him to use his hocks. It will also improve the way you ride corners in canter. Set your four poles down so the centres on the circumference mark the quarters of a clock face, as before, but this time on a 15-m circle. This should give you three energetic but controlled canter strides between each pole.

To make it easier, start by riding over any two poles and go round the others, then as you gain confidence, build up until you are cantering over all the poles in the same rhythm.

Basic grids

Trotting poles to cross pole

Place a pole on the ground 2.1–2.75 m (7–9ft) before a cross pole. If you keep the rhythm of your trot going in, your horse will find it easy to take one trot stride between the pole and the fence and keep a round shape as he takes off.

Once he is used to this, increase the number of trotting poles to three or four. This means the horse has to keep his rhythm and momentum to jump successfully. It's usually better to have a minimum of three poles in a line, as if you have just two, some horses treat them as a jump in their own right.

Cross pole to parallel

Building on the previous exercise, add a pole on the ground 2.4–3 m (8–10 ft) from the cross pole and a small parallel the same distance away. As the horse lands over the cross pole, he should automatically take a canter stride over the pole and should arrive at the correct take-off point for the parallel. You can vary this exercise by having a line of trotting poles rather than a single one.

Adding strides

Now add a small vertical fence 9.6 m (32 ft) behind the parallel. This gives two short strides between the fences and will encourage a round, balanced canter stride and an easy jump.

Schooling satisfaction

Some riders maintain that they and/or their horses find schooling boring. If it comprises trotting round in endless circles, that's not surprising – but that isn't what schooling should be. Schooling should be productive and interesting and whether you want to compete, hack for pleasure or do both, it will improve the communication and therefore the relationship between you and your horse.

Every schooling session should have an aim. It might be to introduce a new idea or it might be to improve a particular area, such as the quality of your transitions or your horse's reaction to your aids. When you take into account time spent warming up and cooling down at the end of each session, you might only spend 10 or 15 minutes doing 'proper' schooling, but you can achieve good work in that time.

Finding a good teacher – or, if you prefer the term, trainer, though the only real difference is that 'trainer' seems to be more fashionable – can boost your enthusiasm and your ideas. Many riders enjoy competing, both as a challenge and as a yardstick of their horse's continuing improvement. Others prefer to ride for pleasure and there's absolutely nothing wrong with either attitude. Unfortunately, some trainers only seem interested in riders who want to compete and look on competition as the be all and end all of everything. However, there are plenty of good ones who get satisfaction from helping any partnership to progress, whatever the rider's aims.

Chapter Eight

Hacking to success

IF YOU WANT TO IMPROVE your horse's way of going, ability to cope with new experiences and general versatility, don't underestimate the value of hacking. Just as importantly, if hacking is the reason you ride and keep a horse, never be reluctant to admit it. There is a tendency for riders to talk disparagingly about themselves – or others – as 'happy hackers' or to say 'I only hack' in the same apologetic way that some women say 'I'm only a housewife' or 'I'm only a Mum.'

Just as being a housewife and mother means you have to master the skills from the domestic to diplomacy, so hacking can be the ultimate challenge for some partnerships. You are no longer within the safe confines of an arena and have to get your horse to listen to you no matter what distractions you meet. Let's face it, the challenge of riding a perfect shoulder-in when in the school is nothing compared to the challenge of using similar techniques to ride past a flapping plastic bag caught in a hedge, or coping when a dog suddenly hurtles down to a gate, barking, as you ride past.

Those who keep their horses in safe hacking country should make the most of it. Of course, for some riders, hacking out from their horse's home is no longer a safe option; if your yard is surrounded by busy roads, you may feel that the risks are too great. If so, make the effort to box up and go to safe surroundings regularly, because both you and your horse will reap the benefits.

Some riders think their horses are far too precious to hack and you may hear them proclaim that they are dressage horses or showjumpers or what-ever, as if competing and hacking were mutually exclusive. But a horse who hacks out regularly gets a wide range of experience that will stand him in good stead at a competition. At one prestigious dressage competition, there were complaints that floral arrangements had been put at the entrance to the arena, because so many horses spooked at them. If you have to cosset your horse to the extent that he can't cope with the sight of two tubs full of flowers, aren't you missing the point of what dressage – which literally means training – is all about?

You can look at hacking from various view-points. It can be something to relax your horse in mind and body, offer you both a change from concentrated schooling and allow you to enjoy being with him and unwind. It should be all these things, but it can also be part of your schooling regime, in a less pressured way. Horses are usually more forward-going out hacking and you can turn quicker responses and extra impulsion to your advantage. It often provides a yardstick for conventional schooling: why be satisfied with a delayed response when you know you can get an instant one?

8.1 *above* Hacking can give you and your horse a chance to relax and unwind.

8.2 *left* As most horses are more forward-going out hacking, it can also act as a yardstick to his responsiveness when schooling.

Bring out the **BEST IN YOUR HORSE**

Safety first

Hacking can only be pleasurable and productive if you can do it safely. With the just-backed horse, this means getting to the stage where you can walk, trot, canter, stop, start and steer without wondering whether or not you're going to get a response.

In this case, and that of any horse you don't know well, or if you've moved your horse to new surroundings, it's sensible to start off with a reliable escort. The key word is reliable and it must apply to both horse and rider; the horse must be reliable in traffic, well-mannered and worldly wise enough to keep going calmly under most circumstances, and his rider must be quick-witted and sensible enough to be able to take the lead if anything unforeseen happens or if your horse suddenly loses confidence. There is no such thing as a bombproof horse, so be happy if you find one who is 99 per cent reliable and has a competent rider with plenty of common sense!

When you're riding on roads and public tracks, it's always sensible to wear high-visibility gear even in good weather. Reflective, fluorescent rider waist-coats and horse boots with the same properties catch a driver's eye whether you're riding down an open road or under trees, and act as an early warning.

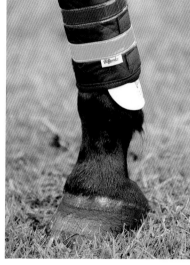

8.3 and **8.4** Reflective, fluorescent rider and horse wear means you can be seen easily, whether on the roads or in woods. It is recommended that riders always wear protective headgear to the highest current safety standards.

Opinions vary on whether or not it's a good idea to hack out alone once a horse has gained confidence. Some people believe you should always go out with at least one other rider so that if anything does go wrong, there is someone who can raise the alarm. I can't argue with this, but at the same time, have found that hacking alone develops a horse and rider's confidence in themselves and each other. It also means that you can tailor the pace and the route to suit yourself; unless you are lucky enough to have a selfless hacking companion, you don't then have to be a killjoy when someone suggests you should have a canter and you feel your horse isn't ready for it.

If you go it alone, be doubly careful about taking standard hacking precautions. Tell someone where you're going and what time you expect to be back – and, of course, carrying a mobile phone.

Schooling whilst you hack

Hacking is a great way of combining work and relaxation, for you and your horse. You can't and shouldn't school as intensively as you perhaps would in an arena – and you must always be aware of what's going on around you so you don't get so wrapped up in the way your horse is going that you don't notice a potential hazard – but you can still achieve a lot.

The first 10 or 15 minutes of a hack should always be spent in walk. The old grooms' rule was always to 'Walk the first mile out and the last mile back' and that's still good advice. Ideally, you should start off asking for nothing more than a regular, active gait. Look on this as your warm-up period before you think about asking a little more.

However, while you should not over-ride your horse, the proviso is that you must always be in control, especially if the early stages of a route compel you to ride on busy roads. Also, if your horse is a bit 'sharp', wherever you are riding you will have to make sure that he is 'between hand and leg' to a sufficient degree so that, if he is spooked by the local pheasant, he doesn't do a 180 degree turn and leave you facing in the original direction. If he is normally a reliable hack but is likely to be fresher than usual, perhaps because he has had a day or two off, it's sensible to lunge him or school him before hacking out.

For the main part of a hack, should a horse be expected to remain fully on the bit? This is one of those questions that can be debated forever; some people say that a horse should be on the bit whenever he's not on a loose rein, but others feel that asking him to stay permanently on the bit when he's not guaranteed to be always on secure footing, and when he's been ridden for relatively long periods is unrealistic and unfair. Steering a middle course seems to work – expect your horse to listen to you and to be what racehorse trainers call 'on the bridle', working forwards into a light, even contact.

Another question that's often debated is whether or not you should trot on the roads as a matter of course. This is a matter of personal preference and safety factors; in the past few years, some councils in the UK have used surfacing materials that do not allow enough traction for horses. However, surfaces that provide sufficient traction may be suitable for short periods of trotting. Keep it short and keep it steady, as concussion jars limbs and feet.

Within the limits discussed above, you can work on many things out hacking that you have been working on in ordinary schooling sessions. Use natural landmarks such as telegraph poles and trees and aim to ride transitions as your shoulder is level with them, just as you would make a transition at an arena marker. Make sure every halt is a square halt and practise riding shoulder-in, turn about the forehand and leg-yielding when appropriate. Use your horse's natural impulsion to ask for a few strides of lengthened trot or canter on good going.

Solving hacking problems

Sadly, some riders don't enjoy hacking because their horses' behaviour makes it an unpleasant, frightening and even dangerous experience. If your horse spooks at every little thing and tries to whip round, gets to the end of the lane and refuses to go any further, becomes uncontrollable when ridden in company or is frightened of traffic, then it's no wonder if you feel tempted to stay within the safe confines of an arena. However, in doing so you're missing out on the chance of enjoying yourself and making it hard to give your horse a varied lifestyle – which may lead to more problems.

Most problems can be solved, given time, patience, a rider with the correct attitude and necessary riding ability and, when necessary, the right professional help. But – and it's a big but – safety must always be your first consideration, both your own and that of other people. The obvious example is that of the horse who is frightened of traffic: there are steps you can take to help overcome his fear, but if you feel there is always going to be a question mark over his confidence, the only safe option is to keep him at a yard with good off-road riding.

You also have to make sure that you are able to give your horse confidence, both by riding him correctly and by staying calm. If your horse is frightened of, say, tractors and you tense up every time you see one in the distance, you're reinforcing his fear. Trainers have always overcome problems like the ones mentioned above by gradually getting horses used to things they are worried about – for instance, giving spooky objects a wide berth, then gradually getting closer – but this process has now been given the label of 'desensitisation'.

Whatever, you want to call it, it works! By breaking frightening or unpleasant experiences down into a form that the horse finds acceptable, then gradually increasing their intensity, you can build his confidence. The following tactics will give you ideas to try and, in some cases, you can carry out 'de-spooking' exercises in a safe environment such as a large school, or in the field.

Although these methods usually increase a horse's confidence, they will not always turn a spooky horse into a 'bombproof' one – not that there ever is such a thing. Some horses will accept unusual things in one environment and still worry about them, though hopefully to a lesser extent, in another.

You also have to remember that horses, like people, get used to being in a particular type of environment and if moved to a different one, can find it challenging to start with – a bit like the townies and country folk scenario! For instance, a horse who has been kept on a busy yard in a suburban environment may be confident with all sorts of traffic, but move him to a quiet countryside home and he may find farm animals terrifying. He needs to be acclimatised and given time to adjust without being put under undue pressure, ideally by being hacked out with a sensible escort. Some horses settle into a new home in a few weeks, but for others, it can take months before they are truly confident.

If a horse spooks at particular objects – perhaps he takes exception to parked cars, or dustbin day is a weekly nightmare – expose him to them at a distance he feels comfortable with, in safe surroundings. If it makes you feel more confident, start by leading him past them on both reins, always positioning yourself between the horse and the spooky object – if he spooks, he'll jump away from it and if you're between the two, you won't get jumped on. Use a 3–3.7 m (10–12ft) rope or lunge rein and a controller headcollar such as a Dually and keep the section between your hand and the headcollar loose, so he doesn't feel restricted. Look in the direction you want to go, not at the object. Once he's happy to pass it both ways, gradually get closer; if he becomes uneasy, move out again until he relaxes, then try again. Eventually, he will go past without worrying and may even want to investigate it. You can then try the same tactics under saddle and finally, progress to hacking out with another horse. When you're out in the real world, riding tactics are important: when you feel your horse tensing up as you approach whatever is worrying him, stay calm and keep your breathing deep and even. Look straight past the 'danger' in the direction you want to go, never at it. Depending on your horse's stage of schooling, turn his head away from the spooky object and keep him going forwards from your inside leg, or ride a true shoulder-in.

Don't hit him, shout at him or keep kicking him, because that will merely reinforce the idea that there is something to be frightened of. Equally important, don't stroke him or pat him as he spooks, because then you're rewarding him for his behaviour instead of giving him the confidence to go past.

If you can't get him past the object and/or you're in a potentially dangerous situation, perhaps because of traffic, get off and lead him past. Some people used to say that doing this was to 'give in' to a horse and would make him spook even more, but ideas have changed. Give yourself time to run up and secure the stirrups – or at least cross them over the saddle – and take the reins over his head. If you are using a running martingale, it's safest to undo the centre buckle of the reins, pull them through the martingale rings and refasten, tying the martingale straps round the neckstrap junction. There may, of course, be situations where you don't have time to do this.

Horses who are frightened of flapping objects can often be helped by a process which trainer Richard Maxwell calls 'sacking out'. Working in a safe environment, start by folding up a piece of plastic until you can hold it comfortably in the palm of your hand, and work it over the horse's body, legs and face as if you were grooming him. Once he is happy with this, unfold it, little by little, until you reach the stage where you can move it over his body, legs and face without worrying him. If at any stage he is worried, go back a step. Eventually – and it will often take several sessions – you will be able to flap the plastic over him without him being worried by it.

Some horses find farm animals worrying, especially if they come towards the horse as you ride past. This isn't surprising: horses are prey animals, so to him, a handful of silly sheep or a herd of curious cows may be potential predators. Again, the best way to overcome this fear is to try to expose your horse to them at a distance, gradually getting closer – but this isn't always practical and you may have to rely on his getting confidence from an escort who isn't bothered by them.

Another tactic that may work, if you can arrange it, is to keep your horse near to farm animals for a little while until he gets used to them. Don't suddenly turn him out with cows or sheep, because he's likely to panic and may bolt through fencing; make sure there's a field between them to start with and, once he has relaxed, move him into a field next to them. This will usually lessen a horse's fear but some animals will always be wary. There are

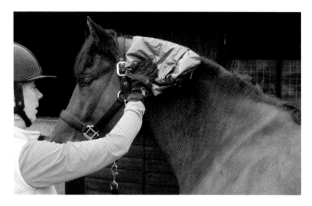

8.5, 8.6, 8.7 The 'sacking out' process, using a piece of folded plastic, may help to desensitise a spooky horse.

also some who grow to accept 'their' cows or sheep but are still frightened of others.

Horses have a keen sense of smell and this often contributes to generating fear. It may be at least partly why so many are frightened of pigs; unfortunately for riders, pigs are intelligent and curious animals and will often run across to have a look at a horse going past. A friend who breeds Connemaras and also runs a pig farm has proved that familiarity does breed contempt, as all his ponies are totally blasé about them – but others are not so lucky.

One tactic that sometimes helps is to counteract a worrying smell. Some trainers believe that a commercial product called Pax helps; described as an aromatic calming fluid, this is applied to the rider or handler, not the horse, and is said to mimic the smell of pheromones that the horse emits when he is calm and safe.

The horse who is traffic-shy often poses the biggest problem, especially if his fear is associated with a previous bad experience. The safest way to try to give him confidence is to turn him out in a well-fenced field next to a busy road, in the hope that being able to set the distance from it at which he feels comfortable will eventually lead to him becoming more secure. This is why New Forest ponies bred on the forest are usually good in traffic.

A horse who is tense but not thoroughly frightened will usually gain confidence if hacked out with a traffic-proof escort, but don't put yourself and others at risk. For many people, it isn't possible to find quiet roads and the only answer may be to find a new home for your horse and, if necessary, a new owner.

Some horses nap out hacking, or when asked to leave the yard, and this is usually an issue of confidence. Most will only nap if asked to go out alone or take the lead and will be perfectly happy behind another horse. This, of course, isn't a situation that can be allowed to continue, as there are bound to be times when you need your horse to go away from his friends.

Although you will often be advised to hit a horse who naps, this doesn't often work. The exception is when a horse or pony is ridden by an inexperienced/ineffective rider and has learned that if he puts on the brakes, his rider can't do anything about it. Even worse, a rider may give up and turn back for home, thus rewarding the horse for his behaviour. If you are sure that the horse is trying it on, recruit a calm, capable rider who can push the horse on and, if necessary, give him a sharp smack just behind the girth the moment he starts 'thinking backwards'.

However, if fear is the root cause of napping, these tactics will only reinforce it. Instead, find someone to hack out with who has a confident, forward-going horse. Start off with your horse just behind his escort then, when it's safe to do so, ride alongside. You can then gradually ease forward until your horse takes the lead; the best time to introduce this is when you're heading towards home, as the horse is more likely to want to go forwards. Don't expect to solve this in one session and don't expect your horse to stride out into the lead: at first, be content if his nose is a little way in front of his companion's.

Another tactic that often works, particularly with a horse who jams on the brakes and/or threatens to rear, is that of waiting it out. However, you can only do this in safe surroundings, where you aren't in danger from other road users or endangering them: don't try this in the middle of a road junction! When you're in a safe area and the brakes come on, just sit there and keep the horse facing forwards. As soon as you feel him taking a step forward, use the verbal command 'Walk on' and stroke his neck or scratch his withers.

If he keeps going, make the most of it. If he only takes one step, or comes to a halt later in the ride, repeat the process. Only try this tactic when you have plenty of time and the patience (or bloody mindedness) to stay with it. UK trainer Heather Moffett, who cheerfully admits that she can be bloody minded with the best of them, was once given a lovely former event horse who napped and reared. She was his last chance, as his owners said that if she couldn't sort out the problem, he would be put down, as he was too dangerous to ride. Heather spent literally all day out hacking and after that, never had a problem; the horse became a valued schoolmaster and was ridden by many pupils.

A horse who is happy to hack out in company but not on his own is showing insecurity. If you never need or want to hack alone, it perhaps won't bother you – but it is a weak link in your communication and you must be sure that your horse doesn't always need to have another one close by as, if you get to that position you can hit all sorts of problems. You must at least make sure that your horse will leave others and work on his own in an arena or field.

Long-reining is often a good way of teaching teach a horse that he must go forwards on his own as well as in company. Start in safe surroundings then, if possible, progress to long-reining around fields, gradually extending the 'comfort zone' away from the yard. If all goes well, you can long-rein on quiet roads and tracks, but make sure you have someone with you to walk at the horse's head and help in case of problems.

If hacking in company – or heading for home on a hack – is something your horse finds exciting, he may react by jogging or pulling. Before you start trying to solve the problem under saddle, make sure he understands the verbal command to walk when being led.

With the horse who starts to jog as soon as he thinks he's heading for home, it can sometimes help to turn him back and walk a short distance. Praise him when he walks, then head for home again. Occasionally, this

8.8 Long-reining is useful for teaching a horse that he must go forwards when on his own, but make sure you are in safe surroundings.

Bring out the BEST IN YOUR HORSE

tactic is counterproductive, but with some horses, the penny soon drops and they realise that if they start jogging, they don't carry on towards home.

Some horses jog habitually because a rider has tried to break the habit by taking a tight hold on the reins. In this case, keep a very light contact and use a neckstrap, coupled with your voice, as a slowing down signal.

Another unorthodox but sometimes successful way of breaking the jogging habit is to get off when the horse starts and walk beside him for a while. A lot of horses who jog whilst being ridden don't do it whilst being led; when he settles, get back on again and if necessary, repeat the process. This is one scenario when mounting from the ground is essential and you have to be able to do it quickly, lightly and without sticking your toe in the horse's side.

Most horses become more forward-going in company, especially when cantering in a group. If you feel you don't have enough control, put group hacks on hold for a while and try hacking out with just one other person who doesn't have the same problem. Sticking to walk and trot, practise riding alongside and when your horse accepts this, changing places so each horse in turn takes the lead.

Don't introduce cantering until your horse accepts this regime calmly and when you do, make sure you're cantering away from home, not towards it. If you can canter uphill, so much the better, as this will encourage your horse to put his back end underneath and not fall on his forehand. At the same time, don't always canter in the same place. This works as a preventive measure, too: if the opportunities to enjoy a canter are sparse, it's tempting to make the most of them and not surprisingly, horses learn to anticipate. If you keep them guessing, sometimes walking a favourite canter route even when the going is perfect, you'll reap the benefits.

There is no shame in using different tack to give you more control out hacking and, of course, different doesn't necessarily mean more severe. A Mailer Bridging Rein is excellent for helping a rider on a strong or excited horse stay in balance and therefore find it easier to keep the horse in balance, without pulling at his mouth. Likewise, if using a pelham or kimblewick instead of the snaffle you use for schooling gives you confidence and helps prevent a tugging contest, use it.

Hopefully, some of the suggestions in this chapter will help you make the most of your hacking or solve problems. However, every horse, every rider and every scenario is different and you have to adapt them to suit your circumstances. Above all, you have to stay safe.

Chapter Nine

Groomed for success

THE PROLIFERATION OF SPRAY-ON coat glosses, shampoos designed to enhance coat colour, products to disguise scars and other cosmetic aids and enhancers tend to make good old-fashioned grooming look as if it's just that – old-fashioned. However, grooming is about much more than looking good: it's also about keeping your horse's skin and coat in good condition, monitoring his health and picking up early signs of problems and spending time with him when neither of you are under pressure.

9.1 Mutual grooming is natural behaviour for compatible horses, as with these two semi-feral Konig ponies.

Literally getting your hands on your horse every day means you become familiar with what is normal for him and can identify any warning signs – such as heat in a limb or a tiny patch of ringworm or mud fever – as soon as they appear. It also allows you to assess how he's feeling, whether he's relaxed and happy to have the attention or switched off and perhaps a bit off-colour.

Most horses enjoy being groomed, as long as it's done in a considerate way. Even those who tend to be aloof rather than affectionate often relax and enjoy it. It's something animals do for themselves and each other; watch two compatible horses in a field and you'll often see the origin of the phrase 'You scratch my back and I'll scratch yours'. Effective grooming is a simple form of massage and, as you'll see later in this chapter, massage and stretches can be incorporated into your grooming regime.

Some people take the attitude that it's not so much what you do to the outside that counts as what you put on the inside: in other words, they believe that a healthy coat comes from feeding, rather than grooming. It's more accurate to say that both are important. Nutrition is vital, but grooming is also important. Apart from the reasons outlined above, it removes dirt and flakes of dead skin and spreads the natural oils in the coat along the hair shafts.

Of course, the appearance of a horse or pony's coat also depends on his type, age, the time of year and the way he is kept. For instance, native breeds naturally grow thick winter coats whilst Thoroughbreds have less natural protection. A thick natural coat is a great insulator because, as the temperature drops, the hairs stand on end and trap a layer of air next to the skin. Although most people rug for the convenience of keeping animals clean and perhaps because they feel guilty if they don't, a lot of animals do a great weatherproofing job on their own.

Although grooming is something that benefits every horse and pony, you need to tailor your routine to your horse's lifestyle. A horse who lives out all the time, isn't clipped and rarely or never wears a rug needs the natural grease in his coat, as it acts as a waterproofing agent. Different horses also have different degrees of sensitivity and the routine you follow and the equipment you use needs to be tailored accordingly. For instance, mares are often more reactive when they are in season and some people believe that chestnuts display greater skin sensitivity than other colours.

9.2 and **9.3** Native ponies' winter coats offer natural protection against bad weather. Compare the Exmoor ponies in their natural habitat in late autumn with the smart ridden Exmoor in his summer coat.

Tools for the job

You may have a packed grooming kit, but are you missing things that make grooming easier and more effective? There are plenty of gimmicks around, but there are also some great ideas. Below are suggestions for basic essentials and useful extras.

Choose grooming tools appropriate to the size of your hand and make sure they are easy to hold. This applies particularly to body brushes, as you need to put your weight behind them. Designs which have soft backs incorporating finger grips, or which are hinged to make it easier to follow the contours of the horse, might cost a bit more than standard wood-backed brushes, but they're well worth the extra.

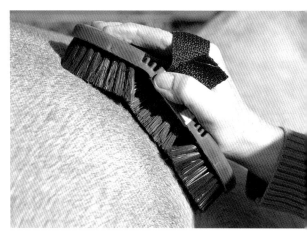

9.4 Brushes with hinged backs make it easier to follow the contours of the horse and work the bristles through the coat.

Every horse should have his own grooming kit, or you could find yourself passing on skin infections. It's important to keep grooming equipment clean; you can't clean up your horse with dirty brushes. Unless the manufacturers' recommendations are otherwise, wash rubber and plastic grooming tools in a bucket of diluted horse shampoo. Plastic-backed brushes with synthetic bristles can also be washed, unless the manufacturer does not advise it. Brushes with leather and wooden backs should not be immersed; instead, dip the bristles in shampoo solution and work them on a clean cloth to remove the dirt.

Large commercial yards sometimes use grooming machines, but although these are effective, they are never as thorough as a hands-on groom. If machines are used, the only way to avoid the risk of passing on possible infections is to use a separate brush for each horse. Some yards prefer to dunk the brush in a solution such as Virkon-E between each use.

Suggested grooming kit

Key items

Hoofpick: designs with shaped rubber or plastic handles are much more comfortable to hold and easier to use than all-metal ones.

Rubber or plastic groomer: These not only remove dried mud and loose hair, but raise grease and dust to the surface of the coat so it can be removed more easily. Most horses love these being used in a circular motion on the neck, withers and quarters. For massage purposes, rubber groomers with pointed prongs are effective but still gentle.

Dandy brush: the traditional dandy with stiff bristles is too harsh to use on all but the thickest coat, but can be used to brush dried mud from unclipped legs.

Whisk or flick dandy: bristles are much softer than a traditional dandy and it is the most efficient and effective way of removing dust and grease from the surface of the coat.

Body brush: choose one with short, dense bristles to make it easier to remove grease from the coat. This is the brush that does the real work, so it's worth paying extra for a good one. Body brushes with padded or flexible backs are more comfortable to hold and so enable you to do a better job.

Metal curry comb: this is used only for cleaning the body brush, never on the horse. Metal curry combs are more efficient than rubber ones for cleaning a brush.

Cotton wool: when you're cleaning eyes and nostrils it's more hygienic to use cotton wool than sponges. By using a separate piece for each eye, you minimise the risk of spreading infection – and why keep germ-laden sponges in your grooming kit when you can throw away pieces of cotton wool after every use?

Fly repellent: gels and roll-on products are safer and easier to use on a horse's face but spray or wipe-on formulae are the only cost-effective way of applying fly repellent over the body. If your horse doesn't like being sprayed, try asking someone to hold him whilst you use a body brush in long strokes down his coat. Alternate a stroke of the brush with a squirt of fly repellent and he'll often accept it, but if this doesn't work, spray it on a dampened and wrung out cloth and wipe it over his coat. This is more economical than spraying the product on to a dry cloth, as less will be absorbed by wet than by dry fibres.

Extras

There are lots of extras that can make life easier. Professional grooms often add some or all of the following to their kits.

Cactus cloth or mitt: made from coarse fibre, this helps to remove stains from a dry coat.

Stain remover product: In foam or liquid form, these can be used as an emergency clean-up measure. Some products need rinsing off whilst, with others, the residue can be wiped off with a cloth.

Headcollar with removable section under jaw: this makes cleaning and clipping a horse's face much easier.

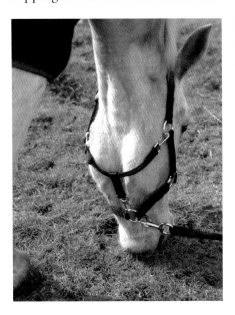 

9.5 and **9.6** A headcollar with a removable section under the jaw makes cleaning and clipping the horse's face easier.

Hairbrush: raid the hair care and beauty counters for a hairbrush with rounded plastic prongs. Used gently, working through sections of hair from the bottom up, this will separate hair without breakage.

Strapping pad: this stuffed leather pad is traditionally used to build up a horse's muscles and stimulate circulation.

Conditioners/de-tanglers: apply to manes and tails before brushing and the job is even easier. Applications last for several days and you can then use a body brush or simply separate hair with your fingers. These products are especially useful for animals with long, full manes and tails, such as native ponies and 'traditional' cobs.

Mane and tail shaping/thinning tools: the traditional way of thinning and shaping manes and tails is to use a metal or plastic pulling comb with narrow gaps between the teeth. If your horse objects to this – or even if he doesn't – there are alternative techniques, as explained in Chapter 10. You'll need a comb with curved blades, originally designed for dog grooming, and a pair of trimming scissors with curved ends.

Sweat scraper: a plastic sweat scraper is kinder than a metal one and can be used to remove excess water after bathing your horse.

Shedder blade: this should be used gently on horses and ponies with thick coats to help remove hair as it is shed. If your horse is sensitive, or has a less dense coat, you can speed up the shedding process by wearing a clean rubber glove and grooming him with your hand.

Plaiting equipment: plaiting bands are useful for securing an unruly mane that you are trying to train over to the correct side in stable plaits. In an emergency, you can also use these to secure competition plaits, but these never look as smart or stay as secure as sewn plaits. For sewn plaits, you need a tapestry needle and strong plaiting thread to match the colour of your horse's mane. As thread is available in a small range of colours, some professionals use tapestry wool to get an exact match.

A matter of routine

Ideally, every horse or pony except those who live out all the time will be given a thorough grooming every day. Realistically, the pressures of work and life may sometimes get in the way and you will have to settle for picking out your horse's feet, checking him over to make sure there are no signs of injury and cleaning dried mud and dirt from areas where tack rests. If time constraints cause a choice between grooming your horse and riding him, there really is no contest!

However, grooming time is never wasted time and in half an hour, you can achieve a lot. Everyone develops a personal routine, but it needs to be logical and thorough, so you aren't missing bits or spreading dirt from one area to another. The following is a suggested work plan.

Run your hands over the horse to check for problems. Pick out his feet and check the condition of his hooves and shoes.

Separate the mane hairs with your fingers, then use a body brush to brush through both sides. When you've done one side, push the mane to the opposite side of the neck and repeat, working from the roots of the hair to the ends.

Unless your horse is clipped, use a rubber curry comb or groomer in a circular motion to remove loose hair and dirt and raise grease to the top of the coat. Tap out grease and dirt that collects in the groomer as you go. Start by working at the neck and go down the shoulder, then move to just behind the withers and work along and down the body. If necessary, and if the horse doesn't object, include the belly area.

When a horse is shedding his winter coat, a rubber curry comb used in a circular motion is a good way of getting out the dead hair. You can also help it on its way by very gentle use of a metal scraper blade; most are plain on one side and have small teeth on the other. The serrated edge makes light work of removing hair, but only use it on a horse who is comfortable with it and don't use it on a horse's legs, face, or belly. Some horses love the feel of a scraper, but others are too sensitive. If your horse objects even to a rubber curry comb, try wearing a rubber household glove and stroking your horse firmly; this will also encourage hair to come out, though isn't as efficient as a rubber curry comb.

Now use a whisky dandy brush to flick off the debris that has accumulated on top of the coat. The secret of success is not just in the design of the brush, but the way you use it – turn your wrist quickly with each stroke to flick away the dust.

You can either brush through the tail next, or leave it until last. If your horse has a full tail, brush through the hairs on the dock, so any dirt falls off – it doesn't matter if it settles on the long hair, because you'll brush it out in the next step.

Separate the tail hairs with your fingers and, if necessary, use a body brush or hairbrush. Start at the bottom of the tail, holding it a little above this point and brushing through to the ends. Gradually work up, a little way at a time, until you reach the dock. Working up the tail in this way makes it easy to separate the hairs; if you start at the top and work down, you'll cause tangles at the bottom.

Now it's time for the hard work, using a body brush to remove grease, stimulate the skin and spread the natural oils in the coat along the hair shafts. To be effective, you need to put your weight behind the brush strokes, so stand far enough away from the horse to allow this and hold the brush in the hand nearer the horse. A lot of people like to work with their dominant hand, especially if they are markedly right- or left-handed, but this forces you to stand in an awkward way when you're on the 'wrong' side – if you're right-handed and use your right hand whilst grooming the horse's left side, you'll twist your body. Not only will this be uncomfortable, you'll be unable to get your weight fully behind the brush strokes.

Again, start at the neck and work to the hindquarters as before, placing the brush on the horse and leaning your weight on it as you make short, sweeping strokes. However, don't put weight on the horse's loins, as this is a weaker area and, as always, be careful when grooming ticklish areas.

Clean the brush after every few strokes by running the bristles over a curry comb, using it in the direction shown in photo 9.8 so you don't cover yourself with dirt – and though it might sound obvious, stand far enough away from the horse so you don't put back the dust you've just removed!

The last parts of your horse to be groomed are his face and legs. Some horses like having their faces groomed, whilst others dislike a brush but are fine if you use your hand. If the bridle has left dried or damp patches of sweat, use a small, damp sponge to clean them. A separate pad of damp cotton wool should be used to wipe each eye.

9.7 *left* Holding a body brush in the hand nearer the horse will enable you to get your weight behind each brush stroke.

9.8 *below* Clean the brush against the curry comb in this direction to prevent covering yourself in dirt and grease.

You can use either a dandy brush or body brush on your horse's legs, depending on his sensitivity. Wet, muddy legs can be left to dry – or you can speed up the process by using leg wraps whilst the horse is stabled – then brushed. Alternatively, you can hose off the mud with cold water, blot up the excess with a towel (without rubbing) and either leave to dry naturally or use leg wraps. You can now buy extra absorbent towels originally developed to allow you to dry your own hair without rubbing it and potentially causing damage; these work just as well on horses and dogs, even if you aren't so worried about split ends!

Personal hygiene

Although there are lots of products formulated for cleaning the sheath of a gelding or stallion, most vets say routing cleaning should be kept to a minimum if the area appears clean and healthy and the horse urinates normally. If there is an excess of smegma, a waxy substance that is the debris from normal secretions, occasional cleaning may be needed.

Use lukewarm water and if necessary, a mild soap that does not contain perfume or colouring. Don't use anything containing antiseptic or detergent, or you could disturb the balance of natural, healthy bacteria and set up infection.

Both genders should have the dock area cleaned regularly with lukewarm water. Some people use a sponge kept separate for this purpose, but the most hygienic way is to use a disposable cloth or pad.

Finishing touches

Want to give your horse a professional finish? Then use a dampened stable rubber – alias a linen tea towel – and wipe over your horse's coat to remove any last traces of dust, working from head to hindquarters in long, firm strokes.

If your horse has a pulled or shaped tail (see Chapter 10) you will need to apply a tail bandage regularly to encourage the hairs on the dock to lie neatly. Dampen the tail hairs, but never dampen the bandage, or it will tighten as it dries.

If you have a cob with a hogged mane, you may see accumulations of grease in it at times when you don't want to give him a bath. The easiest way to remove it is to wipe over the hogged area with a cloth dampened with witch hazel.

At one time, no self-respecting groom would let a horse leave the yard without oiled hooves. These days, hoof dressings are usually reserved for special occasions and range from oils and coloured greases to products incorporating glitter. Sparkling hooves will never be part of traditional turnout, but if you're competing in fancy dress, you might be tempted!

Before using any topical applications, whether for cosmetic reasons or to try to enhance hoof quality, ask your farrier's advice. Some may be beneficial, but others may encourage the hoof to dry out.

Hands-on help

There are useful techniques that can be built into a grooming routine – or used at any other time – to build up your horse's muscle tone and/or help relax unwanted tension.

Wisping or banging

Traditionally, grooms used a technique called wisping or banging – depending on whether it was carried out with a wisp, made from a rope of twisted hay, or a leather pad – to help build up muscles on the neck and quarters. Today, hay and straw is combined into much shorter lengths than used to be the custom, so it's much harder to twist a rope that doesn't fall to pieces as you loop it into a pad.

The leather pads are often described in manufacturers' catalogues as strapping pads; strapping is the old term for a thorough grooming, so perhaps the name originated because their use was a normal part of the routine. They are designed to be brought down sharply on large muscles; as the horse anticipates this, he tenses the muscles, then relaxes as the pad falls. Many horses really enjoy it and will lean in to the pad.

9.9 Regular use of a leather strapping pad can help build a horse's muscle tone.

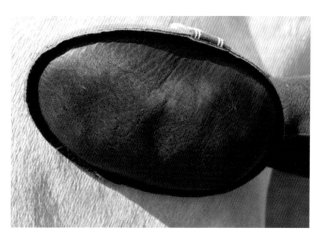

Working muscles in this way helps to improve their tone, but it has to be done regularly; professional grooms reckon that you need to work for 15 minutes, three times a week over three months to get good results.

Massage

Massage is another valuable tool. Of course, grooming is, in itself, a massage in simplest terms, but there are specialist techniques that can be used for promoting relaxation and – when carried out by a qualified practitioner working under veterinary supervision – as part of a rehabilitation programme.

There are many excellent books and videos explaining different massage techniques, but the best way to learn is by attending a course with a qualified practitioner. This is because, although you can learn a lot by reading and watching, you may adopt an incorrect stance or technique. Also, strictly speaking, it is an offence under the Veterinary Surgeons Act 1966 to practise massage on an animal owned by anyone other than yourself without the permission of a vet.

Although massage is non-invasive, there are situations when it should not be used, such as when a horse has lymphangitis or a skin condition such as ringworm. Nor should massage be used to treat lameness, unless by the recommendation of a vet who has examined him.

Massage equipment designed to promote relaxation – and which is sometimes claimed by the manufacturers to have other beneficial effects – is popular with many professional riders and also with non-professionals prepared to pay out the sometimes considerable cost. One of the most sophisticated is the Equissage system, which has been used successfully at World Horse Welfare's Norfolk stables. (This charity was known for many years as the International League for the Protection of Horses.)

9.10 Sophisticated massage equipment in use at World Horse Welfare in the UK, one of the world's leading rescue and rehabilitation charities.

Stretches

Simple stretching exercises that can help loosen up your horse and increase his flexibility can be incorporated into your grooming routine. Some stretches involve extending and retracting the limbs and it really is best to ask a qualified practitioner such as a chartered physiotherapist to demonstrate them to you, rather than guessing at what is required and risking doing something inappropriate and potentially harmful. The stretches should be carried out after exercise, so the horse is already loosened up.

All the exercises should be performed an equal number of times on each side, unless your vet recommends otherwise.

Carrot stretches and belly lifts are the simplest exercises and, because the handler is not physically extending a limb, probably the safest for someone inexperienced to try. Carrot stretches – which are given this name simply because carrots make an ideal encouragement and reward – promote lateral flexion and will show if a horse finds it easier to bend to one side than the other.

Hold your horse on a loose lead rope and position a carrot at his shoulder. This will encourage him to bring his head and neck round to reach the treat; if he tries to 'cheat' by moving his forefeet, re-position him and start again. He'll soon learn that to get the reward, he has to do it properly. If he finds this easy, gradually move the carrot towards his hip so he has to stretch further round.

When we ride, we want a horse to stretch his topline and raise his back. To encourage him to do this from the ground, hold the carrot between his forelegs so he stretches round and down to reach it.

The belly lift is an even more effective way of asking the horse to lift and round his back. Run the ends of your fingers firmly along the midline of his belly, but be careful: some horses, especially those who are ticklish in the belly area, may kick.

As mentioned, some stretches involve extending and retracting the limbs and it really is best to ask a qualified practitioner to demonstrate them to you. However, there is one leg stretch that should be carried out every time you ride and most people probably do it without thinking. That is, of course, stretching each foreleg gently forwards when you have tightened the girth and are ready to mount. Doing this helps prevent skin under the girth and round the elbow area being pinched, but it also helps with general loosening. Don't grab the leg and pull it; ease it forward gently.

Marks of distinction

Quarter marks – patterns made by brushing against the lie of the coat on the hindquarters – are often used on show horses and ponies and some people like to apply them when they compete in dressage. Because they draw attention to the horse's hindquarters and hind legs, they should only be used if he has good conformation in these areas. If he is weak behind, or has less than perfect hind legs, don't use them.

Traditionally, sharks' teeth and stripes are used on hunter types and triangles of small squares are used on fine animals such as show ponies and show hacks. Aesthetically, it makes sense to follow the same guidelines even if you're not applying quarter marks for a showing class, as bold marks suit a larger, handsome horse and smaller ones complement one of fine build.

Use a body brush to make sharks' teeth and stripes. Some people wipe over the coat first with a damp cloth, whilst others prefer to use a damp body brush on a dry coat. You can, if you find it helps, add a little baby oil to the water, but this can tend to attract dust.

To form sharks' teeth, make an upward sweep with the body brush, then a downward one from the same starting point. Follow this with an upward stroke to meet the bottom of the last point down and repeat until you have enough markings. To give a finished look, use your body brush in a downward stroke – straight or curved, depending on which suits your horse – to form an edge. Stripes are made on top of the quarters, using either a body brush or a comb.

The best way to make squares is to use a plastic comb cut to the appropriate size and draw it through the coat to make the patterns. By adding or subtracting a square to every row, as shown in photo 9.12, you can build up a triangle or inverted triangle.

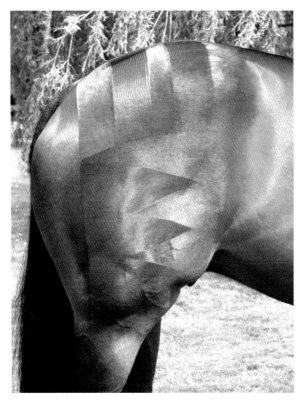

9.11 *left* Sharks' teeth and stripes are made with a body brush and draw attention to powerful hindquarters.

9.12 *below* The best way to make squares is to use a plastic comb cut to the appropriate size.

The marks on one hindquarter should match those on the other, in size and position. Take time to experiment with the way you position them, until you get the effect you want. Once you've got it down to a fine art, you can apply quarter marks shortly before you go in the ring; some people like to apply a fine coat of hairspray to help 'fix' them, but this can also be a dust magnet.

Bathing

Most people like to bath a horse before a special occasion, but unless you're one of the fortunate few with access to a special wash box and drying lamps, you need to adapt your routine according to the weather. In hot weather, when there is no risk of the horse getting cold, it's a straightforward operation, but in cooler conditions you need to do the equivalent of a 'bed bath' to avoid the risk of him catching a chill. If it's really cold, it's unfair to subject your horse to a full bath unless you have the facilities mentioned earlier and you need to restrict yourself to washing his mane and tail and removing stains.

In all cases, get everything ready before you start. Shampoo should not contain detergent, which strips oils from the coat and leaves it looking dull and in some cases, may cause skin irritation: washing-up liquid doesn't suit horses. Choose one formulated for horses, with or without 'coat enhancing' ingredients: the only ones that really seem to make a difference are those designed to brighten white hairs. Some people prefer to use shampoo made for humans, working on the principle that if it's gentle enough to use on your own hair and skin it will be safe for a horse, but if you check the relative costs according to quantity, horse shampoo usually works out cheaper.

Check the manufacturer's instructions for dilution rates and if a product does contain a colour enhancer or brightener and your horse has a sensitive skin, it's a good idea to perform a patch test first. Apply a small amount of the neat product, leave for twenty-four hours and check that there is no redness or flaking.

If you have access to lukewarm water, either from a mixer tap or via a helper who can keep you supplied with buckets, you'll find it easier to both get out the dirt and rinse out shampoo. Cold water closes the pores of the skin, which shouldn't happen if you keep the temperature lukewarm. Don't use hot water, though, or your horse is *more likely* to get chilled.

You'll need to work shampoo into your horse's mane and tail by massaging with your fingers (photo 9.13), but the easiest way to apply it to the body area is with a wash brush (photo 9.14). Designs that have an oval sponge surrounded by rows of short bristles, similar to those on a body brush, are effective: you can use an ordinary sponge, but this tends to work up a lather without getting the shampoo down to the skin.

If you're bathing a horse in hot weather and don't need to keep him partially covered, it's a simple job of working from head to toe. If you are working in cooler conditions, you need to have a rug to hand, ideally one such as a Thermatex, which will wick moisture away from wet hair and skin.

Start by folding back the front of the rug so it covers his back and loins but not his shoulders. Wet the horse's front end with plain water, then apply shampoo to the neck, mane, chest, shoulders and forelegs. When you've worked it into the coat – and, if necessary, left it for a few minutes – scrape off the excess with a plastic scraper, then rinse until all the shampoo is removed. Use the scraper again and towel dry.

Now fold the rug forward and wash the horse's middle section, following the steps outlined above. Finally, adjust it so you can wash the hindquarters and hind legs. You can now position the rug as normal to help the horse dry off whilst you wash the tail. If necessary, you can also use thermal leg wraps to help dry off his legs.

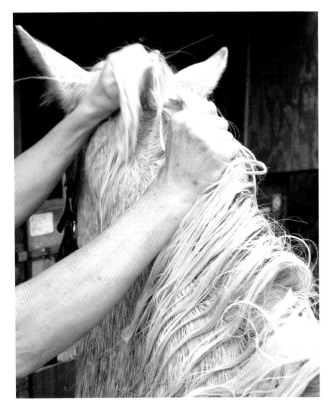

9.13 *left* Work shampoo into the horse's mane with your fingers.

9.14 *below* A special wash brush makes it easier to apply shampoo over the body area.

Bring out the **BEST IN YOUR HORSE**

If you're preparing for a show or competition and leaving early in the morning, you'll need to bath your horse the day before. Using a stretch hood and body – with a turnout or stable rug on top, if necessary – will keep most of him clean, so all you need to do before you leave is wash off any overnight stains on his legs. If he's being stabled overnight and you need to keep his tail clean, cut a leg from an old pair of tights and cut off the toe section. Pull the long tail hairs through the fabric tube, ease it up to the top of the tail and bandage over the top. You can also do this to keep your horse's tail clean whilst travelling; there are special 'tail bags' available, but some horses dislike these and the tights method is usually just as effective as well as being cheaper.

9.15 Using the leg section from an old pair of tights or stockings gives a cheap and easy way to keep a horse's tail clean.

Spot washing

If you have a horse with a fine coat, or one who is clipped, you can use a technique employed in racing stables when it's too cold to bath him. You'll need two buckets of hand-hot water, facecloths or pieces of clean towel and towels for drying him off.

Soak one of the cloths and wring out as much water as possible. Fold back his rug as explained above, then use the cloth in a vigorous circular motion, rinsing it frequently in the other bucket as you go. As you finish each section, dry off the coat with a clean towel before moving on to the next. Some people like to add a tiny amount of shampoo to the first bucket, but it should be much more dilute than the recommended rate for normal bathing.

Light stains can be removed either by using a cactus cloth or sponging the area with a very dilute shampoo solution. There are stain-removing products available, but some are more effective than others.

For last minute clean-ups at special occasions, especially of white face markings, baby wipes can be useful.

Making up

Cosmetic preparations such as spray-on coat gloss are generally accepted, especially in showing, as is the use of a colour product to disguise a minor mark or scar. The exception is if you are showing a horse in a breed class and the use of cosmetic products is forbidden by the breed society; for instance, the Arab Horse Society stipulates that there must be no alteration to the natural colour of the coat, skin or hooves and that the use of oils and make-up should be kept to a minimum. Other societies, in particular those for native ponies, forbid the use of any cosmetics.

All products should be applied sparingly. This applies particularly to oils and colour sprays, as it's far easier to build up the amount you put on than to remove excess. In the showing world, there has been a lot of controversy because so many exhibitors are going over the top, covering ponies' faces with oil and applying black around the eyes and on the hocks of greys. You might need to apply a little more for evening performances under the spotlights, but you still don't want your horse to look like a panda.

The traditional way to keep white socks sparkling is to dust them with French chalk, then brush out the excess. Some manufacturers now offer a similar idea, but with a different application method. Powder is mixed with water to the consistency of yoghurt, then painted on to the white hair. Leg bandages are then applied over clean padding and left overnight whilst the horse is stabled. Next morning, the product has dried and excess powder falls off.

Chapter Ten

Manes and tails

ALTHOUGH DEVOTING A WHOLE chapter to making sure your horse's mane and tail look their best may seem as if you're stepping into the world of My Little Pony, it isn't as frivolous as it might sound. Getting them in the right shape for his breed or type can make a huge difference to his appearance and is an essential part of presenting the perfect picture. It can also help you make the most of his conformation, and simple things like trimming a tail to the correct length or setting plaits at the most flattering angle can make a big difference.

Welfare is, of course, more important than cosmetic considerations. If your horse or pony lives out all the time, you may feel he needs more protection and prefer to leave him with a full tail – which, if necessary, can be plaited for special occasions – rather than pull or shape it. Some people find the practice of pulling manes and tails unacceptable, as they believe it causes discomfort. Whilst many animals don't object, some definitely don't like it; however, there are techniques that can give the same appearance without the need to pull out any hair.

Breed societies and showing organisations have different rules about presentation to which you'll need to adhere if you want to show. These can be a minefield, as guidelines such as those issued by native pony breed societies are often open to interpretation. One person's idea of tidying a mane might be more rigorous than another's and there have been instances where judges have moved animals down the line because they felt exhibitors had gone too far. If in doubt, err on the side of caution.

Fashion may also play a part in deciding how you present your horse and sometimes has a lot to answer for. The obvious example is the way most purebred Arabians, who traditionally have flowing manes, are now shown with long sections clipped off from the base of the ears to, in some cases, as much as 45 cm (18 in) down the neck. The reasoning behind this is that it supposedly shows off the shape of the neck, but it has caused a lot of controversy amongst enthusiasts.

Fashions can be followed or not, but common sense needs to prevail. Whilst some breeds and types are shown with flowing manes and tails, you can have too much of a good thing. There have been cases of horses' tails being left so long that they trod on the ends. Some owners say that these tails can be plaited up or protected by tail bags, but both options leave the animal with reduced defences against flies and biting insects.

If you don't want to show, or don't know the breeding of your horse or pony, you can follow your own inclination. If you do want to compete in showing and performance classes in which turnout specifications vary (for instance, if you want to show a mountain and moorland pony in both breed classes and his height division of a non mountain and moorland working hunter pony classes) you will have to try to make a compromise. You might end up fashioning more plaits than is ideal from a mane you don't want to over-shorten, but most judges will recognise your problem.

Mane attractions

The first thing to decide when tidying a horse or pony's mane is what would be a suitable length and thickness. If he is a native breed and you want to keep within showing guidelines, consult breed society rules and recommendations. You could also look at examples of how ponies are exhibited at top level. Connemaras and New Forests are often shown with their manes about 15 cm (6 in) long but Dales, Highlands, Fells and Shetlands are supposed to have plenty of mane, tail and feather and their manes are much longer.

Look, too, at the shape of the animal's neck and experiment to find a length of mane that suits him. If you want to shorten a mane but aren't sure how much to take off, do it in tiny increments. It might be more time-consuming, but whilst you can always take a bit more off, you can't put it back on.

If you need to plait your horse's mane for competitions, it will need to be about 10 cm (4 in) long and not too thick, or you'll end up with plaits that look like golf balls. A really fine mane can,

10.1 Highland ponies are amongst the breeds shown with full, long manes and tails.

if you prefer, be left slightly longer. You may also need to encourage it to lie flat; traditionally, a mane should lie on the offside of the neck. Some horses have manes which lie perfectly on the nearside, so you need to decide whether to let nature take its course or whether to try to train it over to the other side. Remember, too, that if you pull it or shape it to lie on the nearside and set plaits slightly to the other side, shorter hairs will be on top and more difficult to plait in.

The easiest way to train a mane over to the correct side is to put it in stable plaits. Dampen the mane, divide it into sections, plait each section down to the end and secure with a rubber band. Leave the plaits in for two or three days at a time and repeat the process frequently. Using a Lycra or stretch fleece hood can also help.

10.2 The easiest way to train a mane to lie on the correct side is to put it in stable plaits.

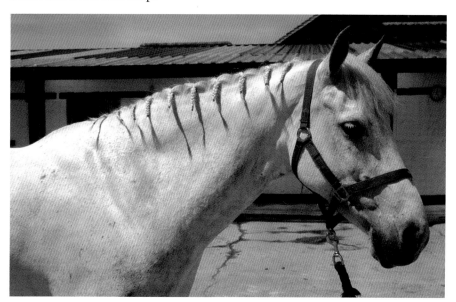

Decide, too, whether you want to cut a bridlepath – remove a short section of hair where the bridle headpiece rests – and if you need to take off any hair at the withers. Some breed societies frown on this, but if you get fed up with parting hair to avoid it getting caught up, you can cheat by cutting a tiny bridlepath, no more than 1.25 cm (½ in) wide. Be careful to position it accurately so it's hidden by the headpiece.

Shaping up

The traditional way to shorten and thin a mane is to pull it, using a metal pulling comb. If your horse doesn't object, there's nothing wrong with this practice, though modern grooming tools make it easy to get the same appearance without the hassle. Traditional pulling is easier, and probably more comfortable for the horse, if you do it when he's been worked and is still warm, as the pores of the skin will be open and the hairs will come out more easily.

Don't wash a mane or apply de-tangler before you pull it, as it's harder to get a grip on clean, slippery hair. Comb it through and decide how much you need to take out to get the same thickness all the way along. Manes are usually thinner near the withers and the hair near the withers and the centre of the neck usually comes out more easily than that nearer the ears. Always take out hair from underneath, as if you take it from the top of the mane you end up with a row of spiky hairs growing out.

Allow plenty of time and, if necessary, pull the mane over several days or try one of the alternative methods below. If your horse gets bored or uncomfortable, he'll throw his head up and fidget. Insisting that you do it all in one go is unfair to him and puts you at risk.

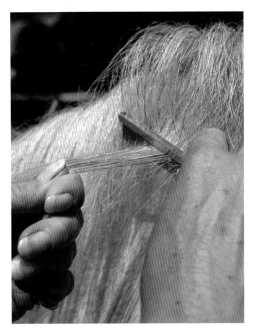

Take a tiny section of hair at a time, push the comb along it to keep the top hairs out of the way – rather like back-combing – and pull out the underneath ones in a quick movement. Hair often comes out more easily if you pull in an upward rather than a downward direction and, if necessary, you can wind the hairs you want to pull out round your comb to give more purchase.

Some people find that the best way to get an even line is to work along the mane, shortening and thinning it gradually, whilst others prefer to complete one section at a time. It's a case of experimenting to find out which method gives you the best results but, in both cases, comb down the mane regularly and stand back to assess your progress.

10.3 When pulling a mane, take out a small section at a time.

Alternative methods

If you don't want to pull out hair, or your horse has such a fine mane that you need to shorten it without thinning it, use a scissoring technique (see photo 10.4). This can also be used to tidy up the bottom edge of a mane that you have thinned, but which is uneven.

For safety, use a pair of scissors with rounded ends. Comb through the mane so it lies flat, without any tangles, then alternately comb and snip at the bottom edge. Hold the scissors at an angle and comb after every cut. This gives a natural finish rather than a blunt edge, or steps.

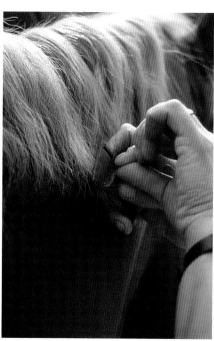

10.4 *left* Use a scissoring technique on a thin mane, or one that has been thinned but needs the edge tidying.

10.5 *right* A clipper blade can also be used to neaten a mane.

You can also neaten the bottom edge by using a clipper blade (removed from the clippers). Back-comb the hair and press down with the blade on the underneath section, nipping off a few hairs at a time.

Another way to thin out a mane is to use a grooming rake with curved blades, originally designed for the dog-grooming industry. Hold it underneath the mane at the crest and comb down, combing through with an ordinary comb at regular intervals to check that you are getting an even thickness along the mane.

Perfect plaits

Plaiting a mane in the traditional style, when appropriate for the animal's breed and type, can enhance head and neck conformation and even give the optical illusion of improving it. Plaiting is essential for some showing classes and is also regarded as putting the finishing touches to your turnout for dressage and hunting. Many people also look on it as acknowledging the time and effort that a dressage judge puts in.

Manes can also be plaited for purely practical reasons. If you have a horse or pony with a long mane that gets tangled in the reins when you are jumping or doing fast work, there are techniques to keep it tidy. These can also be the answer if you want to plait for a dressage competition but are dealing with a mane that is too long and thick for ordinary plaits.

Practice makes perfect, though it might take a lot of practice to achieve a perfectly plaited mane in the twenty minutes that a professional will take to do the job. If you want plaits that will stay in place all day for a competition, you need to sew them with plaiting thread or – if you can't find thread that is the exact match for your horse's mane – tapestry wool in the appropriate shade. It's also best to plait on the day of the competition.

However, if you know you're going to be in a hurry, you can plait the night before. To prevent bits of hay and bedding getting stuck to the plaits, cut the leg from an old pair of tights, cut off the toe and then along the centre to give you a long, narrow rectangle of fabric. Place this along the crest, over the neck and put a band round each plait to keep the fabric in place.

Few horses object to having their manes plaited, though one who dislikes having it pulled might resist until he realises plaiting isn't unpleasant and young horses often become bored with being tied up. As a last resort, you can tie up a haynet, though you'll have to cope with the movement of the horse's head and neck as he pulls out mouthfuls of hay. Most horses are more sensitive near the ears, so it's often best to start at that end before he gets bored and you have two problems to contend with. Try not to brush his ears with your hand or the thread, which will irritate him, and if there are insects about, protect him with fly repellent before you start.

In some respects it's easier to plait in a stable, but this carries with it the drawback that if you drop a needle, you may have to remove all the bedding. It's often safer to tie up the horse outside the stable, as long as you can be reasonably sure he will stand quietly and there aren't too many distractions. Some animals relax more if you leave a radio playing quietly nearby. Talk stations seem to be more soothing than music ones, unless you get an over-enthusiastic presenter.

It's difficult to plait a squeaky clean mane, as the hair becomes slippery, so either wash it a couple of days beforehand or use a spray-on product formulated to give grip on a clean mane without making it look greasy. Unless you are sizing or positioning plaits to suit a particular type of neck conformation, as explained in the next section, comb the mane through and divide it into equal sections of an appropriate number. Traditionally, horses have seven or ninc plaits up the neck and one for the forelock, but most people now accept that there should be as many as suits the horse's or pony's conformation, within reason.

It's often easier to keep sections separate with rubber bands, as this prevents hair from the next section getting caught up as you plait. Dampen the section you're working on, using either plain water or a commercial plaiting product; if you use the latter, shield the other side of the neck with your hand as you apply it to prevent it going over the coat. Divide the hair into three equal sections and keep the plait tight from the base as you work down.

Plait down as far as you can, then secure with a loop of cotton. Pass the needle from the front to the back, then turn over the end and loop the thread round. This tucks the loose ends out of the way and means there is less chance of hairs poking out from the base of your plait when it's finished.

Next, push the needle through the underside of the plait at the neck, double up the plait and then roll it and secure it with two or three stitches. Continue down the neck and if there are any small hairs that are too short to be incorporated into a plait, use a little hair gel to flatten them. Don't be tempted to pull them out because, as they grow back, you'll end up with a row of bristles along the crest.

10.6–10.9 It takes time and practice to achieve a perfectly plaited mane like this one, as demonstrated by show producer Lynn Russell, but the results are well worth the dedication.

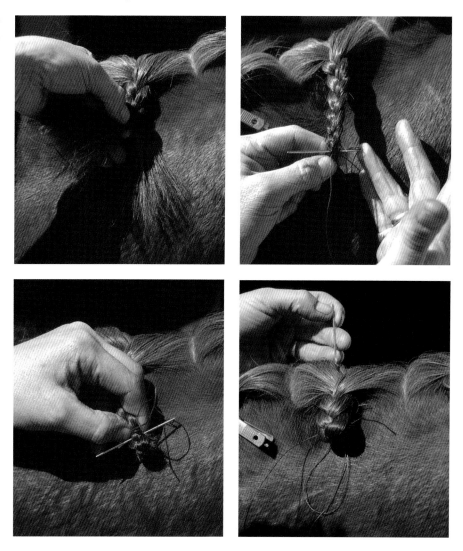

The forelock can be plaited in the same way or, for extra neatness, you can put it in a French plait. This is made in exactly the same way as a tail plait, as explained later in this chapter.

Cosmetic plaiting

If your horse has less than perfect neck conformation, clever plaiting can help minimise faults. On a horse with a weak or immature topline, you can add bulk to the neck by making the first two crossovers of your plait slightly looser than the rest, then keeping the rest taut. When you get to the end of the plait, roll it up so it sits on top of the neck and push back as you stitch so that the plait rests in a hood of hair. If necessary, you can make the plaits along the centre of the neck slightly larger than those near the withers and the ears to increase the effect even more.

If you have the opposite problem of a horse with a thick neck, set the plaits more to the side and don't push back as you stitch them. Give the illusion of extra length to a short neck by putting in more plaits, but don't go overboard or your horse will just look silly. If his neck is noticeably too long, making fewer plaits will 'shorten' it.

Plaiting in itself won't damage the mane hair, but you need to be careful when removing the plaits. The easiest and safest way is to use a dressmaker's

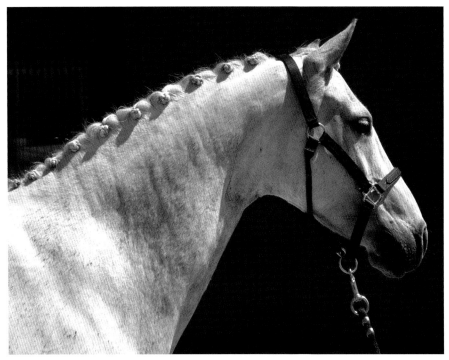

10.10 Setting plaits on top of the neck so that each rests in a hood of hair gives the appearance of a more defined topline.

10.11 Use a dressmaker's stitch unpicker to undo plaiting thread without damaging the mane hair.

stitch unpicker, which you can hook through the thread without risk of the hair being cut.

The only way to find out what best suits your horse is to experiment. This is where rubber band plaits are useful, as they are quick to put in – though they never stay in place as long as sewn plaits and, unless you're particularly dextrous, never look as neat. All you need to do is plait down as before and secure the end with a band, then roll up the plait to the base of the neck and wrap round a second band to hold it in place.

Alternative plaits

At one time, there was a fashion in the dressage world for plaits fastened with white tape. Traditionally, they were only used on Hanoverians competing at higher levels of affiliated competition, but the fashion spread to other breeds. They are still seen on horses at Warmblood gradings and auctions, but in competition, the current fashion is for seven or nine plaits set in hoods of hair. These are often known as 'Anky plaits' or 'Anky rosettes' after the top Dutch dressage rider Anky van Grunsven, who popularised the style.

To make taped plaits, shorten the mane to 10 cm (4 in) and plait down as before. Instead of rolling up the plait, fold it under and secure with white tape or a white plastic clip, both available from saddlers specialising in dressage equipment. Some people like to add the illusion of bulk to a young horse's neck by holding the hair above the crest as they plait, so the finished plait sticks up at an angle. However, unless you to care to get an even line of plaits, this can look rather strange.

'Anky plaits' are made in the same way as conventional ones designed to add bulk to a horse's neck, but are more exaggerated. Start the plait a little below the crest of the neck and push back and stitch as before.

If you have an Arab, native pony or traditional cob with a flowing mane, there will be too much hair to put into conventional plaits. However, if you want to keep it out of the way for convenience or when you feel it's appropriate – for instance, if you're competing in affiliated dressage – a running or Arab plait can look just as smart. Often seen on Arab racehorses, it has a single plait running along the bottom edge of the mane, hence its name.

Comb through the mane to disperse any tangles and take a small section of hair next to the ears as if you were going to make an ordinary plait.

Starting a third to halfway down the mane, make a couple of crossovers, then take in a small piece of mane every time you pass the left-hand section of your plait over the centre.

Continue in this way and, as you work, the plait will curve round and form a neat bottom edge to the mane. When you get to the withers and have no more hair to take in, plait the remaining strands, double up the ends and stitch them.

A Spanish plait, which lies flat along the base of the neck, is made in the same way – but plait tightly from the base and start taking in sections of hair

10.12–10.15 A running plait, as shown on this Welsh Cob, is a practical and attractive way to keep a long mane out of the way.

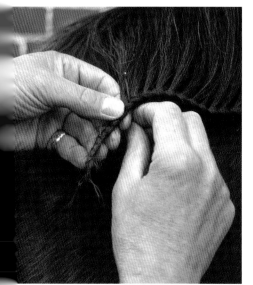

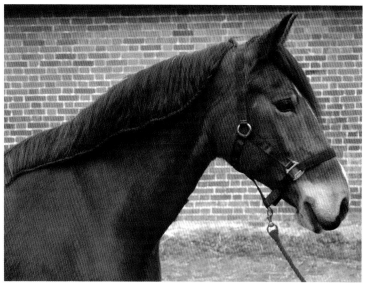

from the left from your second crossover onward (see photo 10.16). Keep your plaiting tight so the braid lies along the crest of the neck. If your horse or pony has an extra thick mane, you can make a double Spanish plait – particularly effective if the hair falls naturally on either side of the neck. Make a centre parting so that an equal amount of hair lies on each side of the neck, then plait each side separately. You'll end up with two plaits lying side by side along the crest.

If you're looking for special effects, perhaps for a quadrille, a lattice plait can look stunning and is quick and easy to make. Divide the mane into small sections of equal size and fasten each one just below the crest with coloured tape. Next, fasten each to its neighbour and if necessary, repeat the process.

10.16 A Spanish plait is made using a similar technique to the running one, but is kept tight so it lies along the crest of the neck.

10.17 A lattice plait gives a decorative effect for special occasions – this horse is being used in a vaulting demonstration.

Hogging a mane

Show cobs and polo ponies traditionally have their manes hogged (clipped off). In the case of cobs, it's done to complement their conformation – a hogged mane often shows off a workmanlike head and powerful neck on a horse who would otherwise look plain. With polo ponies, it's done to prevent the reins getting tangled up in the mane hairs as the ponies twist and turn at speed.

Some people worry that hogging a mane removes a horse's natural protection from insects. It does, of course, but I've never seen a hogged cob look distressed and you can compensate for what you take away by using fly repellent and, when the horse is in the field, a fly mask.

Look hard at your horse before you decide to hog, because if you don't like the result, it will take a year for the mane to grow out. During that time, you'll also have to go through a stage where he looks as if he has a Mohican haircut. One way to get a good idea of whether or not it would suit him is to put his mane in a Spanish plait and push his forelock back under his headcollar.

The only practical way to hog a mane is to use clippers. If the horse has a particularly long, thick mane, it's often easier to cut it short with scissors first, so you don't get skeins of hair catching up in the clipper blades. The professionals' hogging technique is in three confident moves: first run the clippers up the centre, being careful not to cut into the neck hair, then along each side.

10.18–20 Hog a mane by running the clippers down the centre of the neck, then along each side.

As with plaiting, you can adapt your technique to suit your horse's conformation. If your horse has a slightly undeveloped neck and you want to give the impression of more bulk, clip close near the withers and ears but raise the blades slightly in the middle of the neck. With a heavier neck, clip closely all the way along.

Tail endings

The length and shape of a horse's tail also makes a big difference to his appearance. Again, you might need to check breed society guidelines, as some stipulate no thinning or trimming. For instance, the Exmoor Pony Society says that whilst ponies used for driving can have their tails shortened, this is not permitted for ponies shown in ridden or in-hand classes. Purebred Arabs are shown with full, flowing tails that should not be levelled off at the bottom, but because they have a naturally high tail-carriage, length doesn't cause a problem. Some native pony breed societies allow tails to be 'banged' (levelled off) at fetlock level.

In showing classes, the best length of tail for hunters, hacks, cobs and riding horses is usually 5–10 cm (2–4 in) below the point of the hock when the horse is moving. The same guideline applies to show and hunter ponies. To judge how much to trim off, you need to see the horse moving so you can gauge his natural tail-carriage, so get someone to walk him in hand. Once you've decided, ask a helper to put a hand under the dock and hold the tail at the same angle whilst you trim the ends. You can use either scissors or clippers; it's often easier to get a straight edge with clippers, especially on a thick tail.

Many people like to shape a tail at the top and the traditional way to do this is to pull it. Some animals accept this quite happily if it's done considerately – again, the hairs will come out more easily if the horse is warm and the pores of the skin are open – but others don't. It isn't worth taking risks, so either leave your horse with a full tail and plait it for special occasions or use a shaping comb.

Although many people are happy to pull their horses' tails and never have a mishap, it seems to cause more discomfort than does pulling a mane and there is always the risk that you will get kicked. Now that you can get the same result – without the risks – by using a shaping comb, why bother?

These combs are available with coarse or fine blades and are easy and quick to use. Just comb down the sides of the tail with quick, overlapping strokes and on a fine tail, you'll soon get the effect you want. With a coarse

10.21 It's easier to get a straight edge on a thick tail if you shorten it with clippers rather than scissors.

tail, you may need to take a little hair from the centre, as when pulling. Hold up the top layer of hair and comb a little from underneath, then repeat until you have the desired shape (see photos of tail shaping in makeover sequence Chapter 11.)

Whichever method you use to shape a tail, you'll need to bandage it regularly to encourage the hair to lie flat.

Plaiting tails

You may prefer to leave your horse's tail full and plait it for special occasions. It's the traditional method of presenting youngstock for the show ring but professionals prefer to pull or shape their ridden animals' tails. However, the choice is yours and a well-plaited tail can look stunning. It takes practice, and

Bring out the BEST IN YOUR HORSE

to get the best results you need a tail with long enough side hairs to get the plait started – if your horse's tail has been pulled and you're trying to grow it out, you have to be prepared to go through the 'scrubbing brush' stage.

There are two forms of tail plait, one where the plait itself lies flat and the other where it stands out in relief from the side bars. The second is particularly striking, but if you're used to plaiting in the conventional way, you may find that mastering this technique takes practice.

The tail should be clean enough not to harbour specks of grease, but not so squeaky clean that you can't grip the hair. If necessary, use a spray-on product designed to give better grip without making the hair look oily. Start by taking a small section of hair from each side of the top of the dock and cross them at the centre. Next, take a third section from one side and bring it to the centre.

As you plait, take a small amount of hair from each side every time you pass a side section over the centre one. Keep your plait tight, so the side bars stay taut, and only take a narrow section of hair from the side each time; if you take too much, you'll end up with a centre plait that is too thick. If you want the plait to lie flat, pass the side sections over the centre one each time in the conventional way. If you want to create a raised plait, pass them underneath.

Carry on until your centre plait reaches about two-thirds of the way down the dock, then continue it without taking in any more side sections. This will give you a single long plait which can be secured at the end with a needle and thread, doubled up and stitched. Some people prefer to leave it in a loop, whilst others stitch down the length.

10.22–10.28 *here and opposite page* An expertly plaited tail, as shown here, is an alternative to pulling or shaping.

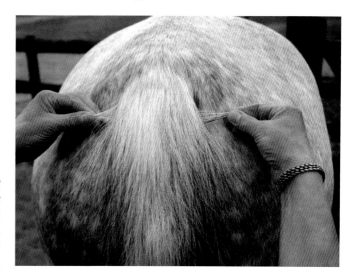

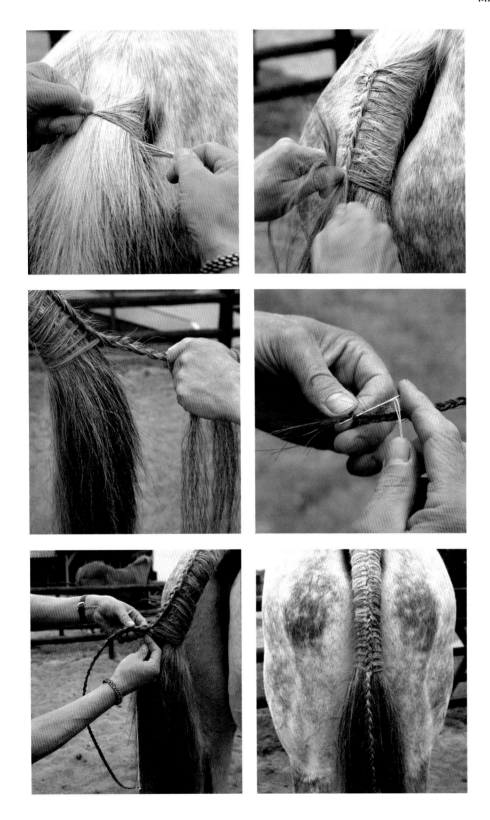

Plaited tails are just as vulnerable as plaited manes. If you have to plait the day before, protect your handiwork with a tail bandage. Be even more careful about removing the bandage than you are putting it on – unwind it, because if you pull it off, you'll wreck the plait.

Filling in the gaps

If your horse rubs a section of his mane, it can make it impossible to create a row of neat plaits. One way of covering up the damage is to roll up the hair that remains into a ball, if it's long enough, and secure it with thread; another is to make a 'hairpiece'.

Take a small section of hair from the bottom of your horse's tail and cut it into lengths about 1.25 cm (½ in) longer than his mane; you need enough to approximate to the thickness of a plaiting section. Using a needle and plaiting thread, bind and stitch one end, then wrap the thread round the short ends of the rubbed section and stitch in place. You should now be able to turn your hairpiece into a plait.

If the rubbed section is near the withers, check the design and fit of your rug. If the rug is too big or cut too deep at the neck, it will slide back and rub. Rugs with built-in neck covers sometimes cause problems, especially if used on horses with high withers. Designs with separate neck covers that fasten to the body of the rug are often less likely to cause problems.

A less common problem is that of the horse who loses the end of his tail, usually because it is eaten by others. If you want to disguise the damage until the tail hair grows down, perhaps because you want to show your horse, it's possible to buy artificial tails that are attached to the remaining hair.

Chapter Eleven

Clipping and trimming

I N THE RIGHT HANDS, a pair of clippers can be a magic wand for a 'before and after' makeover, as clipping and trimming can turn a scruffy hairball on four legs into a super-smart horse. Of course, clipping should be done first and foremost for practical considerations: if your horse or pony copes with his winter workload without getting hot and sweaty, then why take off his coat? In this case, a little trimming of his jaw and legs may be all that's needed to keep him looking neat.

If you do need to clip, don't fall into the trap of taking off all his coat except for that on his legs simply because it seems easier than marking out the lines of, say, a blanket or chaser clip. Always take off as little coat as possible, because it minimises the risk of your horse getting chilled, especially over his back and loins. It's all very well to say that rugs can provide extra warmth, but look at the competitors at any winter dressage or showjumping show and you'll see a lot of horses clamping their tails down and tightening their back muscles as rugs are taken off and riders start literally warming up.

It's surprising how little hair you need to take off to make a difference. If it's your horse's first experience of being clipped, try a bib clip, where hair is removed from the chest, underside of the neck and – if he doesn't object to the clippers on his face – under the jaw and down his cheeks, in line with the bridle cheekpieces. The next step up is a trace clip, which follows the lines of the traces on a driving harness and may be extended to the throat and chest. Next comes the chaser or Irish clip, which can either start at the top of the hind legs and run diagonally across the body to the base of the ears, or become an extended blanket clip. Another favourite is the self-explanatory blanket clip.

You can adapt clips to suit your horse's workload and his conformation. For instance, the extended blanket clip on the Connemara pony in photo 11.1 shows off his well-made front and pretty head but leaves all the coat on his back end. A bib clip (before and after photos 11.2 and 11.3) is enough to prevent a horse in light work sweating on his neck and, extended to the cheeks, shows off an attractive head.

11.1 A version of a blanket clip shows off this Connemara pony's pretty head and good front but leaves protection for his back and quarters.

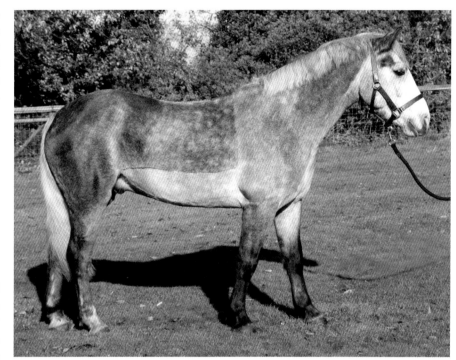

11.2 and **11.3** *below and below right* A bib clip is ideal for a horse or pony with a thick coat, in light work.

Show producers who need to have their horses' coats looking good for early shows usually opt for a full clip as the last one of the season so that there are no lines to detract from their conformation. The grey cob shown in photo 11.4 has had the hair left only on his legs, which have been carefully trimmed.

Tradition dictates that the first clip should only be made when the winter coat has come through fully, in late autumn. However, if the weather is mild, you may need to clip earlier to keep your horse comfortable. Tradition also decrees that the final clip should be made no later than the end of January, for fear of spoiling the quality of the summer coat that may be starting to come through. Having seen horses in professional yards who have been clipped as late as early March and who have grown beautiful summer coats, I've come to doubt this.

11.4 This show cob, about to start the season, has been clipped fully except for his legs – which have been carefully trimmed.

Getting the professional look

Equipment

To get the professional look, you need to have the right equipment and to make sure it is well maintained. Choosing the right clippers means they must not only be suitable for the job, but easy to handle. Whilst professionals who clip lots of horses each season need heavy-duty clippers designed for a tough workload, a one- or two-horse owner will probably be better suited by light or medium weight ones. Take the actual weight of the equipment into account, too. Although modern clippers are lighter than older models, a set of heavy-duty ones can still become tiring to handle if you're doing a large clip.

Battery-operated clippers are often quieter than those which run from the mains, which is important if you're clipping a nervous or inexperienced horse. If you are thinking of buying rechargeable ones, check that they will hold enough power for you to complete the job. Some will only run for about 45 minutes and whilst they may be ideal for a small clip, such as a bib or low trace clip, they might not be up to anything larger. Small trimmers are useful for tidying the head area.

Before you use clippers, read the manufacturer's operating and mainte-nance instructions. This might sound obvious, but a lot of people don't bother. If you make a simple mistake such as not tensioning the blades correctly, you could end up with a worried horse, broken blades or both.

Clippers should cut smoothly, gliding through the coat. If they pull, it means the blades are not tensioned correctly, or are damaged or blunt. Keep the blades lubricated whilst you clip; stop at regular intervals to clean and oil the blades and if you hear the clippers gradually running more slowly, stop immediately. Turn them off, brush out hair from the blades and any air vents, then start them again and apply the manufacturer's recommended oil to the blades. You'll hear them regain speed as they are lubricated, but rest the blades against your hand to make sure they haven't become hot before putting them back on the horse.

If you get into the habit of cleaning and checking clippers every time you use them, and before you put them away, you'll minimise the risk of prob-lems. Get blades sharpened regularly; how often this needs to be done depends on the thickness and condition of the horse's coat as well as the extent of the clip. Always have a spare pair, so if one breaks or goes blunt halfway through a clip you can carry on, and don't mix a blade from one pair with one from another, as they wear to match.

Blades can be fine, medium or coarse. For body clips, fine or medium ones are best; coarse blades are not really designed for use on horses, though they can be useful to trim coarse hair on legs, as explained later in this chapter.

The clipping process

Before you start, make sure everything is in your favour. Trying to clip on a windy day or when other horses are being fed is asking for trouble and it's essential to have a dry area with good visibility where you can stand the horse. If you need to clip him in a stable, take up all the bedding and pile it round the sides so that the hair you take off can be swept out. Take out portable water containers and cover up automatic waterers.

Make sure you have a rug ready to put on and, if you're going to be working at the horse's back end, apply a tail bandage to prevent tail hairs getting caught up. If you're leaving part of the coat on, a dampened stick of chalk can be used to mark out lines and make sure that you don't end up with what looks like a slipped blanket clip. Where the line on one side meets that on the other, such as over the withers, use a piece of string to make sure both sides meet up.

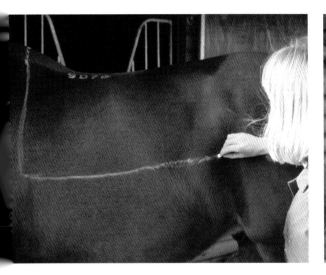

11.5 Mark out the lines of your clip with a dampened piece of chalk.

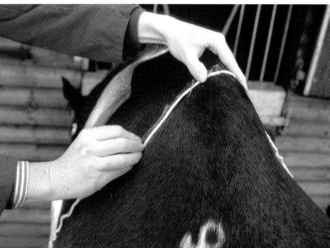

11.6 Use a piece of string to ensure that the line on one side meets the line on the other.

The most frequently asked question about clipping is how to avoid 'tramlines' in the coat and how to create neat edges. If you get tramlines on a horse with a fine coat and are using medium blades, switching to fine ones might solve the problem. What also seems to help is making sure the horse is nice and warm before you start, by using a rug with a neck cover.

If you have a horse or pony with a thick coat, avoiding tramlines isn't so easy. You'll probably have to use medium blades, as fine ones won't cope, but as long as you can make sure he doesn't overheat and become damp with sweat, rugging him for a short time before you start will help. If you do get lines, try going over them in a criss-cross motion.

Professionals often clip out a horse's head completely, including the areas over the eyes and the backs of the ears. If you feel this is essential, it must be done with great caution and if the horse can't be guaranteed to stay calm, you may need to ask your vet to sedate him. Many people prefer not to take the risk of clipping so close to the eyes and either leave a circle of hair round each one or leave the front of the face unclipped. The first method can leave the horse looking like a panda, but the second is smart and safe.

Clip out the jowl and up to the line of the bridle cheekpieces, if necessary using a piece of string to mark out a line from the corner of the mouth to the base of the ear on each side. You can either clip the backs of the ears or leave the hair on. Don't clip all the hair from the inside of the ears, because it gives protection, but you'll find that neatening the outside edges gives a smart, sharp outline. Close the ear gently in your hand and run the clippers up the edges, holding them so the blade is at an angle (see photo 11.7) Some horses don't mind this at all and will stand quietly whilst you use ordinary clippers, but others will only tolerate very quiet trimming clippers. If your horse makes it clear he isn't going to let you anywhere near his ears with any clippers, use a small pair of round-tipped scissors.

Whether or not to clip off whiskers on the muzzle is a personal choice. Some people feel it's essential to give a smart appearance whilst others don't like the idea, as they believe it deprives the horse of a sensory aid.

11.7 *below* Hold the clipper blades at an angle to trim the ears.

11.8 *below right* Use the clippers with the direction of the hair growth if you need to tidy the legs but the horse is slightly light of bone.

Look at your horse's conformation before deciding whether or how to trim his legs. If he has a fine coat, you can often leave the hair on the back of the legs and simply trim off any fetlock hair, using either clippers or scissors and a comb. If your horse is light of bone, avoid trimming down the backs of the legs – or, if they have to be tidied up, use the clippers in a down-ward direction so you are following the lie of the coat rather than clipping against it.

With horses who have coarser leg hair, such as cobs, you'll often find it's easier to get a more natural look if you use coarse clipper blades. To get a sharper look, clip upwards against the lie of the hair unless, as stated, he is slightly light of bone.

Whilst you can't hide major conformation faults, you can disguise minor ones. If your horse is tied in below the knee (has a marked indentation at the back of the knee) don't trim the area closely or you'll draw attention to it. The appearance of small splints can sometimes be minimised by fluffing up the hair around them and using a little hairspray, but you would probably only bother to do this if you were taking part in a showing class.

To add a final neat touch, trim the hair round the coronets. Use small scissors on fine hair and trimming clippers on coarse. If you hold the clipper blades at an angle, you'll get a natural looking finish rather than a 'pie frill'.

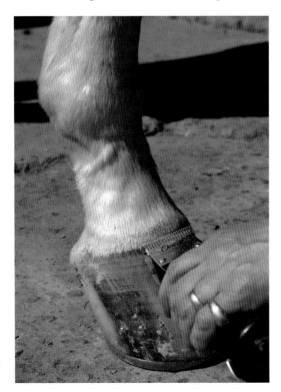

11.9 Holding the clipper blades at an angle to trim the coronets gives a neat finish rather than a pie frill.

Bring out the BEST IN YOUR HORSE

Clipping for conformation

You can design a clip so that it makes the most of your horse's conformation. For instance, setting a blanket clip slightly further back on a short-necked horse can give the illusion of greater length, whilst setting it well forwards can 'lengthen' a short body.

If your horse is narrower through the body than ideal, a chaser or Irish clip will be more flattering than a blanket or trace clip. Alternatively, set a blanket clip high (see photo11.10). You can also flatter a thick neck by running a clip up the neck rather than taking off all the hair so it is visually 'bisected'.

Opinions vary on whether or not you should leave a saddle patch. Most showing people prefer not to, because they feel it detracts from the overall picture. Personally, but with no real evidence to back it up, I'd rather leave the horse with some protection under the saddle no matter what sort of numnah or saddle cloth is used. However, you do need to make sure that it is positioned correctly.

11.10 A high blanket clip has been extended up the top half of the neck on this event horse.

When leaving hair on the legs, the general guideline is to follow the lines of the horse's muscles. However, if his legs are longer in proportion to the depth of his body than is ideal, setting the line slightly lower can be more flattering. Whatever the effect you're trying to achieve, it's worth getting out the chalk first and sketching out some options. You can then decide what looks best before taking off the hair.

Hairy tactics

If you own a native or traditional cob and need to keep the feather on his legs but take off enough coat to enable him to work without sweating, he'll often look best with a bib clip or, if that isn't enough, a chaser one. Blanket or full clips can look rather strange on top of four hairy legs; similarly, if you hog a cob's mane, leaving his feathers on just looks as if you've forgotten to trim them off.

Check breed or showing organisation rules for limitations on trimming. For instance, some allow jawlines to be trimmed whilst others don't. If you have a pony with an unflattering beard under his jaw and can't clip it, gentle use of a grooming rake will give a neater, natural outline.

Show producers in the UK aiming native ponies for the National Pony Society ridden Mountain and Moorland finals at the Olympia Christmas show – one of the highlights of their showing calendar – may give ponies a full clip about three or four weeks beforehand, so the coat grows in enough to look like a summer one. Instead of clipping lines across at the tops of the legs, they often clip down the front of each then taper the clipped section to a V just below the knees and the fronts of the hocks, leaving the hair on the back of the legs. As the hair grows back, it merges in more effectively.

A professional makeover

In the right hands, a pair of clippers can transform a horse, as the photos in the following section prove. Showing professional Lynn Russell demonstrates how she turns Corvus, a novice show cob with the Baileys showing team – just brought in after his winter break – into a smart contender ready to start the season. Some of the points illustrated in these photos have been mentioned in this chapter and Chapter 10 – here, for inspiration, is how a makeover can look when done to professional standards.

The makeover – follow the sequence and see the end result on page 194

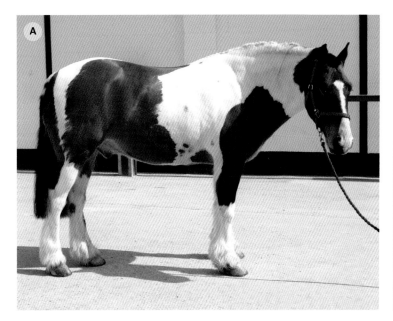

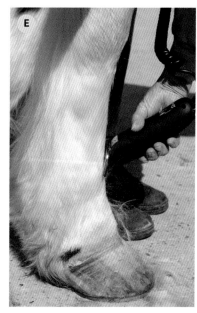

A The basics are all there, but hidden under the hair.

B Hairy legs do not belong on a show cob – the feathers will have to go.

C Lynn uses a spray-on product to make it easier for the clipper blades to glide through hair.

D Starting at the bottom of the leg, she takes off most of the excess hair, using the clippers against the lie of the coat.

E Next, she blends in the remaining hair, this time using the blades in the direction of the hair growth.

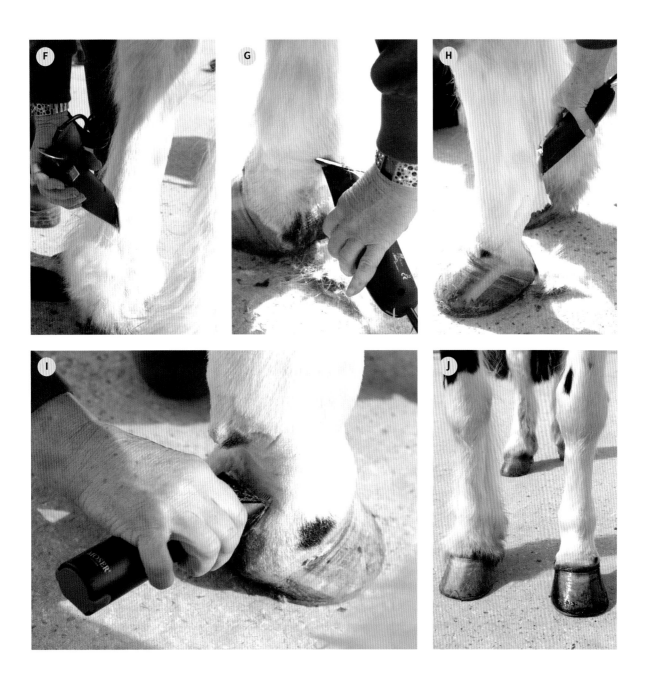

F Taking the clippers down the back of the leg, she gives a clean line to the foreleg.

G, H, I Now it's time to trim and give definition to the fetlocks and heels, changing the angle at which she holds the clippers as necessary.

J Who would have thought these forelegs belonged on the same horse?

Bring out the **BEST IN YOUR HORSE**

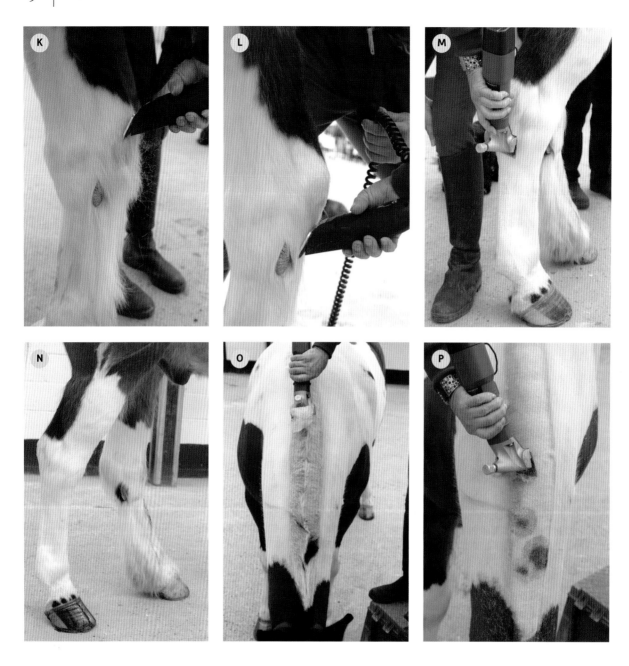

K, L, M Moving to the hind legs, Lynn again trims to give a sharp outline, giving definition to the hock.

N Again, you would never guess that these were a matching pair.

O Hogging a mane is easier if the horse will stretch his neck down to eat from a bucket on the floor – and eating is never a problem with a cob. First, Lynn clips down the centre.

P Next, she clips up each side of the mane in turn. Depending on the horse's conformation, she may clip just before a show – or, if she wants to give the illusion of more topline, a few days beforehand to allow for a little re-growth.

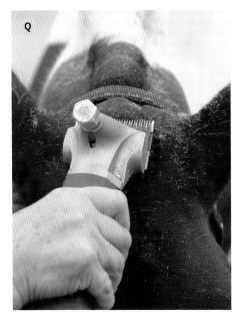

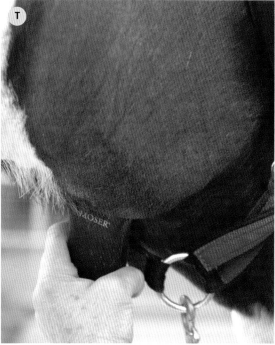

Q The final stage in hogging is to clip the forelock.

R Small clippers are used to trim whiskers. Some people prefer not to do this, but it's accepted practice for the show ring.

S Using larger clippers and small trimming ones helps to create a perfect picture

T Trimming under the jaw gives the neat, sharp outline Lynn requires and shows off Corvus's handsome head.

U Close the ears gently in your hand so you can trim the hair from the outer edges.

V It's easier to get a level bottom edge to a tail by using clippers instead of scissors. Note the correct length of tail for a show cob.

W Strimmed and trimmed and ready to show.

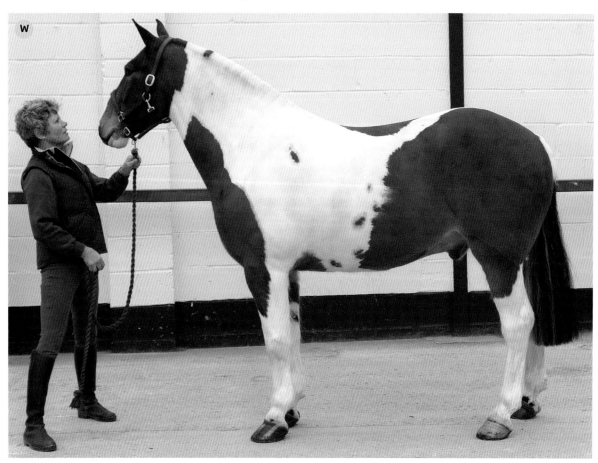

Tail shaping

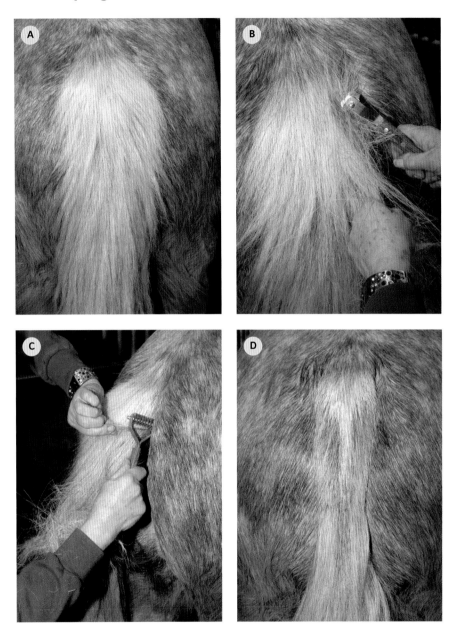

A Corvus's tail was already shaped, but this is how Lynn turns a toilet brush tail into one that shows off a good pair of hindquarters, without the risk of causing discomfort by pulling.

B Take hold of the side hair and comb down with a shaping comb, using short, brisk strokes.

C Hold the top hair out of the way so you can take hair from the sides and underneath of the dock.

D Two minutes later – a perfectly shaped tail.

Chapter **Twelve**

Last word

BY NOW, YOU SHOULD be inspired to take a new look at your horse and your relationship with him. But there's still one piece of the picture to look at – and that's you. To bring out the best in your horse, you need to bring out the best in yourself and make sure that you, as well as your horse, are in good condition, sound and fit!

At one time, even top riders were sometimes guilty of concentrating on their horses' well-being but paying scant attention to their own. But as training for potential international team combinations has, under the umbrellas of national equestrian federations, become more focused, the message is getting through. Riders on Olympic Pathway programmes benefit from advice and hands-on help from experts ranging from physiotherapists to sports psychologists and even those who were at first doubtful of their effectiveness have been converted.

This means that there is growing interest in and acceptance of rider preparation and maintenance filtering through at lower levels. However, it's still common for some riders to assume that whilst such attention to detail is paramount for the élite professionals, it isn't relevant for those who ride mainly for pleasure – which, even when this includes competing, covers most of us.

In fact, it's just as important. If you're tired, stressed, stiff or unfit, you won't ride well or safely. This will at least affect the way your horse goes and the enjoyment you get from your riding and could have more serious effects. When tiredness causes a mistake at a fence which leads to a fall, it doesn't matter whether it's tiredness of horse or rider: you're both at risk and could both be injured.

Assess yourself

Just as you assessed your horse, you need to assess yourself. For a start, are you a reasonable weight for your height? You'll know that without having to stand on the scales, but if you know you're asking your horse to carry more than he needs to, do something about it.

If you want a more scientific guide to your own condition, you might prefer to calculate your body mass index (BMI). This takes into account frame size rather than calculating an ideal weight range according to your height; its one flaw is that it doesn't take into account whether muscle or fat makes up the weight and as muscle weighs more than fat, it can be misleading for people such as rugby players and weightlifters. If you belong in those categories, you'll already know this – if you don't, be honest and don't use it as an excuse!

If you type BMI into an internet search engine, you'll find lots of quick calculators, but it can also be worked out manually. Just find your height in metres, then square it (multiply it by itself). Finally, divide your weight in kilograms by your squared height. As an example, if you are 1.6 m tall and weight 57 kg, the first calculation would be: 1.6 x 1.6 = 2.56. Then, dividing 57 by 2.56 gives a BMI of 22. The accepted BMI scale is:

12.1 Why spend money on going to the gym when you can muck out?

BMI less than 18.5 = underweight

BMI 18.5–25 = ideal

BMI 25–30 = overweight

BMI 30–40 = obese

BMI greater than 40 = very obese

Someone with a BMI at this end of the scale would, fortunately for any horse, be unlikely to ride. The good news is that if you're a rider trying to lose weight, doing what you enjoy will help, as long as it's complemented by a sensible eating plan. It has been calculated that mucking out burns up to 480 calories an hour, sweeping 400, hacking 240 and concentrated schooling 350. It isn't surprising that one enterprising riding school owner persuaded local weight-watchers that helping with the mucking out was far cheaper than going to the gym!

Fit to ride

Are you sound and fit to ride? Chances are that if your horse seems stiff or is moving awkwardly, you'll get him checked out. Do you give yourself the same attention? Normal wear and tear affects the way we hold ourselves and therefore our posture in the saddle and even minor injury can have a major effect.

As an imbalanced rider means an imbalanced horse, you owe it to yourself and to him to get any aches and pains checked out by a qualified practitioner – perhaps an osteopath or chartered physiotherapist who understands the demands riders put on their bodies – and to have a regular check. Sorting out minor problems is easier and cheaper than leaving it until you can't ignore them.

If you own and look after a horse, you probably have a reasonably active lifestyle – but, just as with horses, being fit means being capable of doing a particular job. If you feel fine after a leisurely hack, you're hacking fit, but if you get out of breath or feel tired after a long, energetic ride or halfway round a hunter trial course, you aren't doing yourself or your horse any favours.

If you want to become fitter, there are obviously lots of options, from going to a gym to running, cycling and swimming. What's important is that it must be something you enjoy – or at least don't dislike – so that you'll stick at it. Some people benefit from the support of others and some like to go it alone.

One of the simplest ways of building fitness is also the easiest and cheapest. It's been calculated that brisk walking for 45 minutes a day, four days a week, will improve heart and lung function and, because it is low impact, may also improve bone density. Walking also puts less strain on knee and ankle joints than running or jogging.

Cycling, whether in the open or on an exercise bike, is good for heart, lungs and muscles; if you find it boring to cycle alone, see if your local gym runs a spinning class, where an instructor will take you through a structured programme to music. The real benefit – or punishment, depending on which way you look at it – can come from cycling whilst standing on the pedals. If you enjoy swimming, this can also be beneficial, as you'll be working most of the major muscle groups without putting impact on your joints.

Even if you've never thought of yourself as being a 'gym bunny', find out what your local leisure centre has to offer. For instance, mine runs everything from 'fitness fusion' classes, which combine different forms of exercise to music, to Pilates and yoga. Pilates, which builds core stability, strengthens abdominal muscles and improves balance and stamina, is brilliant for riders in all disciplines and is suitable for all ages. A lot of people who suffer from lower back pain find it helps prevent it and it certainly helps with balance and posture in the saddle.

Although there are many books and DVDs on activities such as Pilates, you won't get the full benefit from the DIY approach. Try to start with a course taught by a qualified teacher who finds out whether you have any health problems – and can therefore make sure that you work at the easiest level or, if necessary, miss out specific exercises – and will lead you through a proper warming up and cooling down routine. You need to practise at home, but qualified instruction means you're practising the right things, not the wrong ones.

Mind games

Are you in the right frame of mind to ride? Being around horses is therapeutic in itself and riding is a great way to put other parts of your life into perspective. Whilst you're riding, even if you're just out for a peaceful hack, you have to be aware of your horse, your surroundings and what you're asking him to do. If you're paying attention to all these, there won't be much room left in your brain for worrying about work or family issues. You may also find that by giving yourself mental time off and concentrating on other things, you allow your mind time to come up with answers and solutions that previously eluded you.

In fact, it's your duty to your horse to make sure that whenever you spend time with him, whether riding or looking after him, you focus your attention on him. Horses pick up on their owners' physical and mental tension, so teach yourself to close a mental door on anything that is worrying you before you approach him.

If you've had a bad day or are facing a difficult one, take slow, deep breaths, inhaling through your nose and exhaling through your mouth. Raise your shoulders as high as you can, then roll your shoulder-blades down and round several times. Find what Pilates instructors often call the 'neutral spine'; stand with your feet the width of your hips apart, place your hands on your hips and tip your pelvis forward, then back, then find the position in between. This is your neutral spine, or centred position.

Take a deep breath in, then roll down to 'lengthen' your back muscles. Nod your head and let your arms hang loose in front of you as you think about letting your body roll down, one vertebra at a time, as you breathe out.

Only go down as far as is comfortable, then come up in the same slow, measured way, finishing by shrugging and rolling your shoulder-blades as before. These simple exercises are a great way to loosen muscles that often get tense, especially if you've been sitting at a desk or driving, but they also help to relax you mentally.

Are you setting yourself reasonable goals and priorities? As we've already shown, it takes time to achieve results when you're trying to improve your horse's way of going, so break down your riding goals into a series of stepping stones and if your goals are set in terms of competition, judge your progress by comparing your performance against your own previous ones, not those of other people. For instance, it doesn't necessarily matter what your dressage score is compared to that of the winner: what's important is whether you are making progress in terms of the way your horse goes and behaves.

Do you have the right attitude, or are you setting yourself up to be shot down? If you're always telling yourself that you're a 'rubbish rider', you won't allow yourself to make progress. Similarly, make sure that anyone who helps you offers constructive, not destructive, criticism. Lessons should help you and your horse improve and teachers should be encouraging; if you finish every session in the depths of despair, give yourself a chance and find another teacher!

In conclusion

Hopefully, this book has shown that whatever type of horse or pony you own, and whatever you enjoy doing or aim to do with him, there are lots of ways to take a new look at him and make the most of him. In doing so, you should forge a strong relationship with a new horse or improve the one with a horse you own already.

This may be enough to help you achieve your aims, whether they lie in competition, riding for pleasure or both – or even to show you that you can achieve even more than you thought possible. For some riders, trying to get the best from a horse may show that, no matter how hard you try, there will always be a fundamental incompatibility between what you want to do and what he is capable of; it may be that his natural capabilities lie in an area which doesn't interest you and it isn't fair to ask him to be a square peg in a round hole. But whether you continue to progress in this partnership, or move on to another, you'll find that making the most of your horse is an enjoyable and rewarding challenge.

12.2 Bring out the best in your horse and your relationship with him will be even better.

Bring out the BEST IN YOUR HORSE

Further reading

Devereux, Sue, *The Veterinary Care of the Horse* (ed. Karen Coumbe), J.A. Allen (London) second edn. 2006.

Diggle, Martin, *The Novice Rider's Companion*, Kenilworth Press (Shrewsbury) 2009.

Henderson, Carolyn, *Getting Horses Fit*, J.A. Allen (London) 2006.

—— *Horse Tack Bible*, David and Charles (Newton Abbot) 2008

Henderson, Carolyn, and Coumbe, Karen, *The Horse and Pony Care Bible*, Ebury Press (London) 2007.

Henderson, Carolyn and John, *All About Bits and Bridles, Allen Photographic Guides*, J.A. Allen (London) 2000.

—— *Clipping, Allen Photographic Guides*, J.A. Allen (London) 1996.

—— *Grooming, Allen Photographic Guides*, J.A. Allen (London) 2007.

Henderson, John, *The Glovebox Guide to Transporting Horses*, J.A. Allen (London) 2005.

—— *Towing Trailers, Allen Photographic Guides*, J.A. Allen (London) (revised edn.) 2006.

Jago, Wendy, *Solo Schooling*, J.A. Allen (London) 2003.

Lilley, Claire, *Schooling With Ground Poles*, J.A. Allen (London) 2003.

—— *The Problem-Free Horse*, J.A. Allen (London) 2007.

MacLeod, Clare, *The Truth About Feeding Your Horse*, J.A. Allen (London) 2007.

Mailer, Carol, *Better Jumping*, J.A. Allen (London) 2008.

Moffett, Heather, *Enlightened Equitation*, David and Charles (Newton Abbot) 1999.

Van Laun, Richenda and Loch, Sylvia, *Flexibility and Fitness for Riders*, Allen Photographic Guides, J.A. Allen (London) 2000.

Index